Acknowledgments

The authors would like to thank the following people for their contributions to the development of the *W.A.G.E.S.* curriculum:

K. Daniels, consulting teacher

Sally Mann, consulting teacher

Jim Creech, general manager, Northwest Stamping, Business Advisory Board

Tim Stokes, owner, Metal Products, Business Advisory Board

Chris Rolfe, manager, Western Pneumatics, Business Advisory Board

Ron Keebler, owner, Oregon Gallery, Business Advisory Board

Naomi Rombaoa, University of Oregon, student intern

Chuck Lange, consulting teacher

John Connolly, consulting teacher

Jim Fryback, consulting teacher

Helen Fast, consulting teacher

Linda McKenzie, consulting teacher

Gail Lang, consulting teacher

John Lee, consulting teacher

Susan Dodrill, consulting teacher

Mike Michel, consulting teacher

Linda Atwood, consulting teacher

Chris Reiersgaard, consulting teacher

Diane Jeffcott, consulting teacher

Mike Tedesco, consulting teacher

Leo Batenhorst, consulting teacher

Vince Suetos, consulting transition specialist

Elyse Myers, consulting transition specialist

Brandi Starck, consulting transition specialist

Jeri Dickinson, Ed. Consultant

About the Authors

Michael D. Johnson has spent over 28 years working in the field of special education, dealing with students from 12–21. His experiences have focused on building prevocational and vocational social programs for a broad range of disabled students. Michael has spent more than seventeen years working with behaviorally disturbed (BD) students and families in his local school district in Springfield, Oregon. His familiarity with agencies that support BD students includes working relationships with vocational rehabilitation and juvenile counselors, mental health caseworkers, and corrections/parole officers. He also works as a technical assistance coordinator at the University of Oregon, providing expertise and support to teachers, administrators, and adult agency staff throughout the state who are involved in a nationally recognized school-to-work program, the Oregon Youth Transition Program. His association with university staff working in the field of transition culminated in the publication of the *NEXT S.T.E.P.* curriculum, a practical approach to empowering students in the transition process. He has also coauthored articles for nationally recognized journals on alternative strategies for delivering services to disabled students. He has presented at local, state, and national conferences targeting best practice transition models in special education. Michael's knowledge as a practitioner makes him a reliable resource to school districts, state level management teams, and adult service providers throughout the state of Oregon.

Michael Bullis earned his Ph.D. in special education and rehabilitation from the University of Oregon in 1983, specializing in research methods. He is also a nationally certified rehabilitation counselor. Before returning to the University of Oregon in 1995, he was a research associate at the University of Arkansas' Rehabilitation Research and Training Center on Deafness, and the associate director of the Teaching Research Division of Western Oregon University. Since 1986, Dr. Bullis has been awarded and has managed 30 externally funded research and model demonstration projects focusing on high-risk adolescents.

Michael R. Benz primarily focuses his teaching and research on secondary education and transition practices and postschool services and outcomes. Before coming to the University of Oregon, he was a high school special education and social studies teacher. He has also taught in alternative education settings, working with at-risk youth, high school dropouts, and older students returning to school to complete their education. For the past 12 years he has codirected Oregon's Youth Transition Program, a nationally recognized school-to-community transition model that has been implemented in over 175 high schools throughout Oregon. In 1999, Dr. Benz received the Oliver P. Kostoe award from the Division on Career Development and Transition, Council for Exceptional Children, for outstanding national contribution to the advancement of career development and transition.

 **Keith Hollenbeck** has been working in education for the last 24 years. His experiences range from primary education to collegiate teaching and from general or regular education to special education. His doctorate is in special education with an emphasis in curriculum design and assessment. Keith currently works for Springfield Public Schools and the University of Oregon. In Springfield, he is an administrator in the Department of Student Services, Special Education. Besides large-scale statewide assessment research and district-wide curriculum-based assessment, Keith also places an emphasis on institutionalizing empirically validated effective curriculum design, teaching practices, and assessment procedures into the district. At the University of Oregon, Keith is a research associate in the College of Education, Behavioral, Research, and Teaching (BRT). Prior to his work in BRT, Keith was associated with Dr. Doug Carnine and the National Center to Improve the Tools of Educators (NCITE) in curriculum design, assessment, and in-service issues.

Contents

Appendix

PART ONE

Instructor's Guide

Introduction

The *W.A.G.E.S.* instructor's guide contains two major sections. The first section, **Curriculum Overview and Teaching Strategies**, provides information on the content of the curriculum, the format imbedded into each lesson, and strategies for implementing the curriculum with students. The second section, **Conceptual and Research Foundation for the *W.A.G.E.S.* Curriculum**, provides information on the rationale for the content included in the curriculum, and the social skill and instructional design principles that served as the research foundation for the curriculum.

Each section of the guide complements the other section. The first section provides practical information related to specific implementation of the curriculum, while the second section provides conceptual information related to the design of the content and format of the curriculum. We believe that a clear understanding of both sections will help the instructor deliver the curriculum in a more knowledgeable and effective manner.

Curriculum Overview and Teaching Strategies

This section gives you the information you need to effectively deliver the *W.A.G.E.S.* curriculum and will also give you a better understanding of how to utilize the curriculum so that the nine-week course of study is more motivating to students. Strategies for implementation are divided into the following areas:

- ◄ Lesson Format
- ◄ Complementary Activities
- ◄ Teaching Tips
- ◄ Evaluation and Assessment

LESSON FORMAT

W.A.G.E.S. contains 33 lessons, each designed to be taught within a 40- to 50-minute class period. The 33 lessons and the complementary activities that accompany them easily provide enough content to fill a nine-week term. The body of the curriculum is divided into the five sections given in **Table 1**.

Table 1: Summary of *W.A.G.E.S.* Curriculum Content

SECTION	CONTENT	LESSONS
UNIT ONE	INTRODUCTION	LESSONS 1–2
UNIT TWO	LOCUS OF CONTROL	LESSONS 3–8
UNIT THREE	TEAMWORK	LESSONS 9–13
UNIT FOUR	COMMUNICATION	LESSONS 14–24
UNIT FIVE	PROBLEM SOLVING	LESSONS 25–33

Each lesson is designed with the following format:

- ◀ **Purpose:** A brief explanation of why each lesson is being taught and the concepts to be covered.

- ◀ **Learning Outcomes:** What students will be able to accomplish as a result of each lesson.

- ◀ **Review:** A brief recap of the previous lesson.

- ◀ **Required Materials:** The supplies and equipment necessary to effectively complete each lesson.

- ◀ **Vocabulary:** Any new words or phrases that will be introduced in each lesson. Explanation of the new word or phrase should be worked into one of the lesson's activities.

- ◀ **Description of Activity:** An explanation of how to conduct activities associated with each lesson.

- ◀ **Wrap-Up/Homework:** An opportunity to summarize each lesson and assign additional activities.

Table 2 presents the scope and sequence of the entire curriculum and provides a quick reference tool for understanding how all the pieces fit together. The complementary activities that support the four major units account for nine additional days and may be facilitated in conjunction with events and curricula already in place within any educational setting. These activities represent career awareness and matching endeavors, job search and marketing experiences, and extended learning opportunities in the community.

Table 2: *W.A.G.E.S.* Curriculum: Scope and Sequence

SECTION	LESSON	COMPLEMENTARY ACTIVITIES	LESSON TITLE	ASSESSMENTS
UNIT ONE	1		Getting the Ball Rolling	CBM Vocabulary Test #1
	2	CAREER GUIDANCE ACTIVITIES	*W.A.G.E.S.* Program Overview	
UNIT TWO **LOCUS OF CONTROL**	3	INTEREST INVENTORIES	Locus of Control = RESPONSIBILITY	
	4	CAREER APTITUDE ASSESSMENTS	What Does "Locus of Control" Mean to the Team? (Part One)	
	5	JOB MATCHING	What Does "Locus of Control" Mean to the Team? (Part Two)	CBM Vocabulary Test #2
	6	(1–2 DAYS)	Self-Control (Part One)	
	7		Self-Control (Part Two)	
	8		Making More *W.A.G.E.S.*	Unit One Mastery Vocabulary Test
UNIT THREE **TEAMWORK**	9		Teamwork	
	10		Good Values Are Out of This World!	
	11		What's in the Bag?	
	12		What's in a Team?	CBM Vocabulary Test #3
	13		Practice Makes Perfect	Unit Two Mastery Vocabulary Test
UNIT FOUR **COMMUNICATION**	14		Did I Hear You Right?	
	15		Communication Breakdown	
	16		Could You Repeat That?	
	17	RÉSUMÉ	Accepting Criticism	
	18	COVER LETTER	Communicating With Power	CBM Vocabulary Test #4
	19	LETTER OF APPRECIATION	Communicating With Self-Control	
	20	EMPLOYER MOCK INTERVIEWS	Enthusiasm	
	21	(5–6 DAYS)	Peer Interviews Orientation	
	22		Interviews With Peer Ratings (Part One)	
	23		Interviews With Peer Ratings (Part Two)	CBM Vocabulary Test #5
	24		Interviews With Peer Ratings (Part Three)	Unit Three Mastery Vocabulary Test

Table 2: *W.A.G.E.S.* Curriculum: Scope and Sequence *(continued)*

Section	Lesson	Complementary Activities	Lesson Title	Assessments
Unit Five **Problem Solving**	25	**Job Shadow** **Or** **Industry Tour** **(1 Day)**	How Do I Solve the Problem?	Problem-Solving Pre-Test
	26		Let's Solve Some of Our Own Problems	
	27		Dependability	
	28		Honor Role	
	29		The Whole Is Greater Than the Sum of Its Parts	
	30		Creative RADD	
	31		Making More *W.A.G.E.S.* Again	
	32		Let's RADD Our Problems (Part One)	CBM Vocabulary Test #6
	33		Let's RADD Our Problems (Part Two)	Unit Four Mastery Vocabulary Test Problem-Solving Post-Test

COMPLEMENTARY ACTIVITIES

The *W.A.G.E.S.* curriculum includes several activities that complement the 33-lesson package. **Table 3** provides an explanation of how and why these activities are woven into the instructional design. At some point during the Unit Two instruction, students will spend a full day utilizing their school's career center, the Internet, or another resource that will allow them to participate in some form of career assessment. Likewise, during the Communication Unit (Unit Four), students will spend three full days designing a résumé, cover letter, and letter of appreciation (following the interview) to complement the interview activities. Two to three additional days will be necessary for students to participate in the employer mock interview that is recommended as an assessment activity for Unit Four. And, finally, a community-based activity that allows students to explore a work environment within their career interest area is a recommended addition to Unit Five. This activity may be an industry tour to a large group or a student may act individually as a "job shadow." The purpose of such an activity is to provide a hands-on experience that more fully develops a student's understanding of his or her career interest area.

Table 3: Summary of Activities That Complement Curriculum Lessons

ACTIVITY	DAYS	RATIONALE	WHAT WORKS BEST?
CAREER GUIDANCE (Unit Two)	1–2	Provides a career focus and a vocational context for the course of study.	Utilize your school's career center to help students gain awareness of the types of careers in which they may be interested. Use of the Internet may also provide interest inventories and career matching that allow for a career focus.
RÉSUMÉ DEVELOPMENT (Unit Four)	1	Demonstrates career focus and markets students' strengths, abilities, and interests. Prerequisite for the employer mock interview.	Most high schools have existing résumé software programs that can be useful in designing a résumé. The Internet and some word processing programs may also have résumé templates that will be helpful.
COVER LETTER (Unit Four)	1	Introduces each student's interest in a particular career field.	Utilize high school computer lab to compose a form letter.
LETTER OF APPRECIATION (Unit Four)	1	Provides students with an opportunity to thank community patrons who participate in the employer mock interview for their time.	Utilize high school computer lab to compose a form letter. Have students ask for the business card of the employer who interviews them.
EMPLOYER MOCK INTERVIEW (Unit Four)	2–3	Provides a realistic interview where students can demonstrate skills learned during the communication unit.	Work with other school staff to host a major event that brings community businesses into the learning environment.
JOB SHADOW/ INDUSTRY TOUR (Unit Five)	1	Allows students to discern the relationship between the employment skills taught in the curriculum and the workplace. Provides additional opportunity for students to demonstrate their communication skills.	Reward students for engaging in this career exploration activity on their own time.

TEACHING TIPS

The *W.A.G.E.S.* curriculum was field-tested over a period of five years in multiple learning environments with different teachers and student groups. The curriculum was revised over time, based on student achievement measures and satisfaction surveys, teacher assessments of student learning, and evaluation information about the effectiveness and usefulness of the curriculum collected through focus groups with students and teachers. As part of this curriculum development process, we recorded specific suggestions from teachers and students about how to successfully motivate and engage students in all lessons and activities. These teaching tips are summarized in **Table 4**.

Table 4: Teaching Tips From Practitioners and Students

LESSON	WHAT WORKS?	WHAT DOESN'T WORK?	POSSIBLE STRATEGY
LESSON 1: GETTING THE BALL ROLLING	A panel that is representative of both white-collar and blue-collar careers in the community is important.	Students don't understand the reason they are taking the first Curriculum-Based Measurement (CBM) test. It is very difficult.	Carefully explain that the purpose of the CBM testing is to show growth and improvement over time.
LESSON 2: W.A.G.E.S. PROGRAM OVERVIEW	Play the "Making W.A.G.E.S." Contest and limit choices to 100- and 200-point questions to establish vocabulary.	Not introducing the unit vocabulary list. Not reviewing the list of workplace qualities generated in Lesson 1.	Systematically introduce vocabulary at the beginning of the lesson.
LESSON 3: LOCUS OF CONTROL = RESPONSIBILITY	Have students generate vocational or social dilemmas that have been handled with "moaning" or "owning" behaviors.	Students often don't want to record internal or external locus of control responses for homework using the LOC Log.	Create incentives that reward tracking locus of control at home or on the job.
LESSONS 4 & 5: WHAT DOES "LOCUS OF CONTROL" MEAN TO THE TEAM?	Engage the entire class in this activity so that everyone has a role (e.g., create a panel of judges, a scorer, clearly defined roles on each team).	Poor management tactics if the class is large (25–30 students). Weak facilitation will not produce a high level of participation from each team.	Pick a student who is capable of being a good facilitator and prepare him/her to conduct the game.
LESSONS 6 & 7: SELF-CONTROL	Get students to feel comfortable offering examples of those words, statements, or actions by others that tend to set the student off.	Poor capability in facilitating an open discussion. Too much attention to worksheets and not enough to discussion.	Put more energy into the facilitated discussion before assigning the worksheets. Make the worksheets a team activity.
LESSON 8: MAKING MORE W.A.G.E.S.	Have all the materials ready to go before students arrive (e.g., game cards, score cards, recording template on blackboard).	Don't allow students to skip the game and miss out on critical vocabulary.	Spend some time on the front end reviewing Unit One vocabulary.
LESSON 9: TEAMWORK	Make this activity as competitive as possible. (This has been a very popular activity.)	Failure to set hard and fast rules that govern competition.	Make sure that all rules are clearly understood by all teams.
LESSON 10: GOOD VALUES ARE OUT OF THIS WORLD!	Make sure that all team members feel that their opinions matter.	Characters in the activity tend to be too blasé and fail to promote heated discussion.	Spice up the appeal of the characters by altering their personalities to stimulate discussion.
LESSON 11: WHAT'S IN THE BAG?	Have every team member play a part in the skit.	Poor time management so that there is too little time for each team to perform its skit.	Strictly enforce the time for each skit. Use a kitchen timer, if necessary.
LESSON 12: WHAT'S IN A TEAM? **LESSON 13:** PRACTICE MAKES PERFECT	Students should be wearing appropriate clothing that allows for movement and flexibility.	Group lacks leadership and communication.	Make sure that there is leadership in each group.
LESSON 14: DID I HEAR YOU RIGHT?	Preparation for this activity needs to be taken seriously so that objects and items are duplicated for each pair.	Not having the time to fully explain the activity so that it generalizes to work, school, or social settings.	Tightly monitor time spent on each task (e.g., use a kitchen timer).

Table 4: Teaching Tips From Practitioners and Students *(continued)*

LESSON	WHAT WORKS?	WHAT DOESN'T WORK?	POSSIBLE STRATEGY
LESSON 15: COMMUNICATION BREAKDOWN	Have students strive to be active listeners and clearly articulate what they hear.	Students not taking their role seriously (e.g., not listening, messing up the phrase on purpose, not whispering softly).	Attempt to determine where the breakdowns occur and who might be responsible.
LESSON 16: COULD YOU REPEAT THAT?	Make sure that good and bad examples of paraphrasing are modeled.	Don't send students off to do the worksheets without clearly modeling the desired outcome.	Get two students to effectively model paraphrasing to the class.
LESSON 17: ACCEPTING CRITICISM	Clearly articulating to students the importance of being able to accept criticism.	Don't go straight to the worksheet without a clear explanation of its purpose.	Role-play some examples of social interactions that are threatening and would cause students to become defensive.
LESSON 18: COMMUNICATING WITH POWER	Help students understand the relationship that "I" and "You" statements have on being passive, aggressive, or assertive.	Don't go straight to the worksheet without a clear explanation of its purpose and use. Poor facilitation of a discussion.	Role-play several examples of passive, aggressive, and assertive communication.
LESSON 19: COMMUNICATING WITH SELF-CONTROL	Be very familiar with the activities within this lesson prior to beginning class. Students like the clarity that the props (chairs) provide for their respective roles.	Don't rush through this lesson or assume that all of the content has to be covered in one session.	Extend this lesson over two days if students need more time with the content or if they need or want more time with the activities.
LESSON 20: ENTHUSIASM	The more enthusiastic the teacher is about this lesson and the importance of seeing the "bright side" of the problem, the more successful the activities will be.	Students may not be able to generate their own slogans that demonstrate hope and optimism. Facilitating this activity with pairs of students within teams of eight may be difficult for some students.	Provide each eight-member team with a staff member who is knowledgeable about the assignment.
LESSON 21: PEER INTERVIEWS ORIENTATION	Direct, clear instructions will establish the amount of "buy-in" students will have for the next three lessons. Make sure that students understand what the expectations are for the next three days.	Not utilizing a direct instructional technique to undertake this orientation. Not providing a good example of the role-playing that will occur over the next three lessons.	Be prepared for the orientation. Choose students who will be able to clearly model an effective interview.
LESSONS 22, 23, 24: INTERVIEWS WITH PEER RATINGS	This is a highly charged activity. Students are easily motivated when playing the role of interviewer or interviewee.	Students not being validated for evaluating their peers during the interviews.	Make sure there is ample time for students to fill out the evaluation forms and discuss weaknesses and strengths of the interviewees.
LESSON 25: HOW DO I SOLVE THE PROBLEM?	Select a "humorous" example of a problem that can be easily broken down utilizing the RADD technique. By sharing a personal experience of problem solving, the teacher allows students to see him or her as fallible.	Too much instruction and not enough interaction will make this lesson too dry and unmotivating. The RADD formula by itself is threatening to students with an aversion to the written word.	Allow students a great deal of flexibility when recording their RADD observations. Don't insist on complete sentences and grammatical clarity.

Table 4: Teaching Tips From Practitioners and Students *(continued)*

LESSON	WHAT WORKS?	WHAT DOESN'T WORK?	POSSIBLE STRATEGY
LESSON 26: LET'S SOLVE SOME OF OUR OWN PROBLEMS	Reward students for bringing in examples of their own problems. Allow them to simply tell their stories, even if they aren't recorded.	Again, too much instruction and not enough interaction.	Validate students by recording their comments on the board. Simply handing in the RADD Worksheet falls short.
LESSON 27: DEPENDABILITY	Teacher-led discussion of each example that is offered in "Paint Me Dependable."	Not supporting students who struggle to read the four vignettes and respond with a RADD Worksheet.	Provide a problem-solving support group for students who may desire to have the vignettes read aloud and then respond orally.
LESSON 28: HONOR ROLE	Teacher-led discussion in answering each honesty/dishonesty statement.	Simply handing out the worksheets and not effectively modeling responses.	Support students who may require assistance in reading the vignettes and completing the RADD Worksheet.
LESSON 29: THE WHOLE IS GREATER THAN THE SUM OF ITS PARTS	Preparation, Preparation, Preparation. Rehearsing this activity beforehand will pay big dividends. Materials need to be assembled beforehand.	The roles that different members of the team are assigned may create some confusion and undermine the activity.	Try doing the exercise without the assignment of specific roles (e.g., using a blindfold, no talk, etc.)
LESSON 30: CREATIVE RADD	The paper bag skits are the strength of this lesson. Help students select a theme.	Tying the props to the theme may create some confusion. If the props don't lend themselves to the role-play, things could go south.	Allow students to select props that they would like to use, rather than confining them to using what they are dealt.
LESSON 31: MAKING MORE W.A.G.E.S. AGAIN	Allow students to facilitate this last game. Let them alter the rules in any way they want.	Too much of the "same old" game may create boredom or lack of engagement.	Provide some sort of incentive/reward for those scoring above a certain level.
LESSONS 32 & 33: LET'S RADD OUR PROBLEMS	Make sure that each team is clear about both doing effective role-playing and providing an explanation of the RADD process.	Too much role-playing and not a clear explanation of how RADD was utilized in the presentation.	Divide the role-play into a presentation segment and an explanation segment.

EVALUATION AND ASSESSMENT

The *W.A.G.E.S.* curriculum utilizes two forms of assessment to evaluate student progress. The first type of assessment is a Curriculum-Based Measurement (CBM) that occurs before the first lesson and then again throughout the program. Each of the six CBM assessments is designed to sample student proficiency of unit vocabulary at various stages during the course of study. Students are introduced to vocabulary that they are not expected to know, but, over the course of *W.A.G.E.S.*, they come to recognize the terminology associated with the concepts taught in the curriculum, the first step in understanding those concepts. CBMs are used as indicators of conceptual understanding and growth as the curriculum is rolled out. Evidence from earlier field tests shows that these measurements have historically improved as students become more familiar with the terminology associated with each unit.

The other type of evaluation utilized within the curriculum is mastery assessment. Each of the four units has culminating mastery tests that reflect mastery knowledge of terminology presented within each unit. Mastery is also assessed in Unit Three by utilizing peer ratings on job interviews. This is followed by a mastery assessment during the employer mock interview. Unit 4 utilizes a pre- and post-test mastery format to assess proficiency in solving problems within the workplace as they are presented in various vignettes.

Table 2 shows when the assessments should occur. The CBM tests, unit mastery tests, and employer mock interview evaluation are included in the Appendix to the curriculum.

Conceptual and Research Foundation for the *W.A.G.E.S.* Curriculum

Finding a job and working successfully are two of the hallmarks of being an adult in our society. The benefits that work can provide in terms of money, self-direction and fulfillment, life structure, and "position" within our culture are central to the way in which individuals—as well as others—view themselves. These experiences also act to shape the subsequent opportunities and the life-course an individual will follow (Osipow, 1983).

There is also no question that being successful in terms of finding, securing, and maintaining an appropriate and meaningful job is one of the major goals of virtually all gifted, average, at-risk[1], or disabled adolescents in our country (Benz & Kochhar, 1996; Crites, 1989). Most gifted and average adolescents will succeed in finding, maintaining, and advancing in work as they leave school and enter the community, but the same cannot be said for adolescents who are at-risk or who have disabilities.

Employment as an explicit outcome for adolescents with disabilities was articulated in the federal Transition Initiative, which began in the middle 1980s (Will, 1984). In line with this initiative, hundreds of research projects have been conducted to document and profile the way in which these adolescents leave public school and enter the community, examining specifically their employment experiences (Rusch, 1995). In 1985, the Office of Special Education Programs funded the National Longitudinal Transition Study (NLTS) (Blackorby & Wagner, 1996; Wagner, 1992), a longitudinal project involving a nationally representative group of students with disabilities and designed to profile the transition experiences of adolescents with disabilities. Results from the NLTS and other projects focusing on states or regions (e.g., Benz, Yovanoff, & Doren, 1997; Bullis

---

[1] We use the term "at-risk" to refer to adolescents who engage in any, or all, of the following behaviors: criminal acts, substance abuse, serial sexual relationships, and school failure. This usage is consistent with the research done by Donovan and Jessor (1985).

& Yovanoff, 2002; Bullis, Yovanoff, Mueller, & Havel, in press; Hasazi, Gordon, & Roe, 1985; Sitlington, Frank, & Carson, 1992) paint a bleak picture of the employment-related transition experiences of adolescents who are at-risk or who have disabilities:

◀ Unemployment among most adolescents with disabilities who have been out of high school for two to four years ranges from 30 to 40%, *more than twice that of their peers without disabilities.* The *highest* unemployment rates are exhibited by adolescents with emotional disabilities—upwards of 50 to 60%. Adolescents who exhibit extreme antisocial behaviors display unemployment rates of 60 to 70%.

◀ Compared to peers without disabilities, adolescents who are at-risk or who have disabilities tend to work: (a) longer at entry-level positions; (b) fewer hours per week and at a lower wage; (c) without benefits; and (d) in jobs that do not advance to higher paying jobs.

◀ In the years immediately following high school and compared to students without disabilities, adolescents who are at-risk or who have disabilities tend to: (a) "drift" among entry-level type jobs and (b) have a high percentage (20 to 40%) of jobs end by termination.

◀ The dropout rates for adolescents with learning disabilities or who have emotional disabilities is high—on the order of 30 to 60%. It appears that the great majority of adolescents who display antisocial acts tend to disengage from school and to not complete school.

◀ Engaging in successful and structured work experiences while in high school is associated with working successfully after leaving the public schools. Stated differently, if an adolescent can be offered different work experiences through secondary/transition programs while in school, it is more likely that he or she will work successfully after leaving school.

◀ Only a few adolescents with learning disabilities (about 30%) or emotional disabilities (15 to 20%) will enroll in any type of postsecondary education. Adolescents displaying antisocial behaviors also tend *not to enroll in postsecondary instruction* after leaving public school.

The (a) overall poor employment experiences after leaving high school of adolescents who are at-risk or who have disabilities and (b) the fact that most either do not complete school successfully and/or do not go on to enroll in postsecondary education, begs the question: "What can be done to improve the employment success of students with disabilities—particularly those with emotional disorders or who would be considered as at-risk?" Although there is no one simple answer, it is apparent that instruction offered to adolescents in secondary/transition programs is apt to be the last coordinated and comprehensive intervention many will receive prior to entering the community and adult life. It is thus essential that these interventions be structured in the most powerful and effective manner possible.

Work that has been done to develop such programs shows that these interventions must include community-based work placements and focused, school-based instruction to promote and support adolescents' transition and employment success (Benz & Lindstrom, 1997; Bullis & Fredericks, 2002). In particular, social skill instruction should be a central component of secondary/transition programs (Kohler, 1993), especially for adolescents with emotional disabilities or at-risk behaviors, as these groups generally demonstrate the types of social behaviors that employers are less likely to tolerate (e.g., talking back, failing to ask for assistance, etc.).

The research literature is clear that *social competence* (an external evaluation of an individual's abilities to interact with others) or, more precisely, *social skills* (the specific behaviors exhibited by an individual when interacting with others) are a major variable differentiating successful from unsuccessful people (McFall, 1982). A number of studies suggest that adolescents who are at-risk or who have disabilities are less socially skilled compared to "typical" peers (Dishion, Loeber, Stouthamer-Loeber, & Patterson, 1984; Freedman, Rosenthal, Donahoe, Schlundt, & McFall, 1978; Gaffney, 1984; Gaffney & McFall, 1981; Henderson & Hollin, 1983; Parker & Asher, 1987). Adolescents who are at-risk or who have disabilities tend to lose their jobs because they cannot—or do not—display appropriate social interaction skills with their work supervisor or coworkers (Bullis, Fredericks, Lehman, Paris, Corbitt, & Johnson, 1994; Bullis, Nishioka-Evans, Fredericks, & Davis, 1993; Chadsey-Rusch, 1990; Cook, Solomon, & Mock, 1988; Griffiths, 1974; Parker & Asher, 1987).

Because of the importance of job-related social skills to the employment success of adolescents with disabilities and those who are at-risk, it is surprising that there are few research-based instructional curricula designed to improve social behavior in competitive work settings for adolescents (Bullis, Walker, & Sprague, 2001; Chadsey-Rusch, 1990). Further, at least one study documents that transition and vocational professionals do not, in general, conduct social skill training in standard and/or consistent ways (Sacks, Tierney-Russell, Hirsch, & Braden, 1992). There is then a pressing need for a curriculum for adolescents who are at-risk or who have disabilities that (a) addresses job-related social behaviors in an effective manner, (b) is pragmatic in design so that it can be used in school settings, and (c) utilizes instructional approaches that are as powerful as possible.

The last point about instructional approaches deserves some discussion, as, to date, social skills interventions have not amassed a positive record as an effective long-term intervention (Gresham, 1997, 1998; Shamise, 1981). Generally, criticisms regarding social skill training approaches have focused upon: (a) the lack of specificity of the instructional content (e.g., the social skills that are targeted are too general to be applied in a specific setting—in this case, the work setting); (b) the fact that many social skills curricula tend not to embody and use effective instructional methods; (c) curricula often are either too brief or too weak to effect meaningful social skill changes among adolescents with clear social skill deficits; and (d) many social skills curricula are too complicated and/or unsuited for use in school settings, which dictates that professionals "adapt" those materials and thus weaken the instructional approach.

Given the social skill deficits that many adolescents with disabilities or who are at-risk display in general and specifically in the work setting, and the weaknesses of current social skill training approaches and curricula, there is a pressing need to develop an effective and relevant curriculum to train adolescents with disabilities or who are at-risk for competitive job placements. This fact is what fueled our efforts to create the *W.A.G.E.S.* (Working At Gaining Employment Skills) curriculum.

We have worked for more than five years to develop, refine, and evaluate this instructional package to be sure that it is effective, practical, and enjoyable for both adolescents and teachers. The *W.A.G.E.S.* curriculum is designed to be taught in the secondary grades with average, at-risk, and disabled adolescents in roughly half a semester. It can also be used with homogenous groups of adolescents (e.g., all at-risk adolescents in a correctional setting). The evaluations we have conducted on the impact of the *W.A.G.E.S.* curriculum on adolescents suggests that average, at-risk, and disabled students learned and improved in each unit and that the three groups of students performed in similar ways on the curricular measures we have developed. This indicates that even those youth with emotional and behavioral problems can be taught to perform in a manner that is roughly equivalent to that of "average" peers. In the sections that follow, we discuss social behavior and the theoretical model we followed in developing the *W.A.G.E.S.* curriculum. We also address the concept of job-related social behavior.

Social Behavior: General Orientation and Theory[2]

In developing the *W.A.G.E.S.* curriculum we used a cognitive-behavioral orientation, as this approach has demonstrated the strongest and most durable effects for at-risk and disabled children and adolescents (Ager & Cole, 1991; Lochman, 1992; Marzillier, 1980; Meyers & Cohen, 1990; Schumaker, Pederson, Hazel, & Meyen, 1983; Urbain & Kendall, 1980). Further, this approach made intuitive "sense" to us and was consistent with the recommendations made by employers with whom we have worked, who commented repeatedly that they wanted workers who could "think for themselves."

Social behavior is regulated through both cognitive and behavioral processes (Bandura, 1986; D'Zurilla, 1986; D'Zurilla & Goldfried, 1971; Meichenbaum, 1977). Simply put, it is necessary to *know how to behave* in social interactions *in order to perform* in the most effective possible way in social interactions. Furthermore, it is widely recognized that social interactions are governed, in large part, by the context in which they occur (Kazdin, 1979; McFall, 1982). What is expected in terms of behavior in a competitive job may be totally foreign to the great majority of these adolescents. This point underscores the importance of understanding the critical skills necessary to succeed in the job setting. The following quote speaks to the importance of content specification in social skill training efforts:

> Many fundamental questions concerning the underlying assumptions, concepts, and methods of the skills training approach have been ignored. Some investigators, for example, have developed the content of their skill-training programs without first conducting a thorough and systematic analysis of the performance problems supposedly addressed by the programs. As a result, they have no way of knowing whether their programs actually focused on the most relevant problem situations for their clients or whether the behaviors taught in the programs represented genuine solutions to these target problems . . .. (Freedman et al., 1978, pp. 1148–1149)

---

[2]This section borrows heavily from McFall's article on the reformulation of social skills (1982) and has been used in previous publications (Bullis, Tehan, & Clark, 2000; Nishioka & Bullis, 2002; Bullis, Walker, & Sprague, 2001).

Further, it is widely believed that adolescents with emotional disorders and those considered at-risk exhibit thinking errors that contribute greatly to their inappropriate behaviors (Henggler, 1989; Kazdin, 1987).

Figure 1 presents a visual display of the cognitive-behavioral process. Interested readers should review the seminal writings on this theoretical model for more in-depth treatment than is possible here (Bandura, 1986; D'Zurilla, 1986; D'Zurilla & Goldfried, 1971; McFall, 1982; Meichenbaum, 1977).

Figure 1: The cognitive-behavioral process

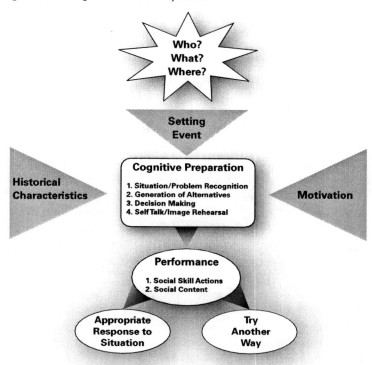

The first step of the social behavior process has been labeled, variously, *problem recognition, situational analysis, roletaking,* or *empathy* (Eisenberg, & Miller, 1987; Eisenberg & Strayer, 1987). In this step, the individuals involved in the interaction interpret the context in which the interaction occurs and then discern subtle nuances surrounding that exchange, whether from reading nonverbal cues from the other person in the interaction or from interpreting the prevailing mood of that individual. Of specific relevance to adolescents with emotional disorders or at-risk behaviors is the way in which they interpret a social interaction; their interpretation is based, in large part, on their histories and personal characteristics. Thus, a person who has a history of being treated harshly or of acting aggressively in other social interactions is more likely than peers without such histories to attach negative connotations to a seemingly benign event (Chandler, 1973; Dodge, 1980; Dodge, Price, Bachorowski, & Newman, 1990).

After this initial "sizing up" of the situation, it is important for a person to generate a number of possible solutions or behavioral responses to the presenting interaction, a process called *generation of alternatives.* From this array of alternatives, the individual then chooses what he or she believes to be the best possible response to the interaction, a step called *decision-making.* In the final cognitive step, the individual performs a *mental rehearsal* of what he or she will do to implement and perform that response alternative. Various studies suggest that children and youth with emotional disorders or judged as at-risk will evidence deficits across these three interrelated processes (Dodge & Frame, 1980; Dodge & Newman, 1981; Platt, Spivack, Altman, Altman, & Seizer, 1974).

Following this cognitive preparation to behave, the individual will perform the alternative, or the behavioral response, to the presenting social interaction. The behavioral response will consist of two observable components: the social skill mechanics and the social context of the response.

Social skill mechanics are the ways in which the individual expresses the content of the interaction (e.g., smiles, gestures, body movements). They represent subtle nuances of social interactions that can greatly color and influence the other person's interpretation of the behavioral response. Two studies concerning job-related social behavior deserve mention.

The first study (Spence, 1981a) examined the social skills that differentiated 18 criminal offenders from a matched sample of 18 nonoffenders. Interviews were conducted with all subjects and included a role-play interaction with the interviewer. All of the interviews were recorded on videotape and then rated by six judges on two areas: (a) overall social competence (friendliness, social anxiety, social skills performance, and employability) and discrete social behaviors—skills that we have chosen to call social skill "mechanics" (e.g., fidgeting, eye contact, smiling), and (b) the manner in which something is said or transmitted to another person. Offenders scored significantly lower than nonoffenders in all areas. Five discrete social behaviors were correlated to the employability rating for the offender group: latency of response, eye contact, amount spoken, head movements, and smiling. The second study (Spence, 1981b) followed similar procedures with a sample of 70 male criminal offenders. As before, components of overall social competence (friendliness, social anxiety, social skill performance, and employability) and discrete social skills (e.g., fidgeting, eye contact, smiling) were rated. In this process, four social skill mechanics were identified as critical to employability ratings: initiating conversation, eye contact, smiling, and fluency (speaking in an unbroken sequence).

Finally, the *social context* of the response is what is actually said or performed in relation to the presenting situation. The effectiveness of the response—whether it is appropriate or not—will be a judgment that depends in large part upon the impressions of some third party. For example, in a job setting, such a judge might be a supervisor, or in a living situation, it might be a roommate, spouse, or landlord. These judgments may vary depending on who the judge is (e.g., supervisors may view the same behavior very differently from different coworkers) and where the behavior occurs (e.g., behaviors in a production setting may be judged differently than behaviors in a break room or eating area).

After the behavior is performed, the person committing the behavior should *analyze the consequences* of the initial behavioral response and, if necessary, reformulate another response to the presenting interaction. Of course, it is entirely possible that the response to the presenting situation will produce a variation to the situation—essentially creating another situation—that must also be responded to.

FOUNDATION OF THE *W.A.G.E.S.* CURRICULUM

We developed, evaluated, and refined the *W.A.G.E.S.* curriculum over a five-year period in the Springfield, Oregon, public school system. We adopted the cognitive-behavioral approach as the foundation of the *W.A.G.E.S.* curriculum and took steps to address each of the deficiencies in most social skill curricula we mentioned earlier: (a) the lack of specificity of the instructional content; (b) failure to use effective instructional methods; and (c) curricula that often are either too brief or too weak to effect meaningful social skill changes or are too complicated or unsuitable for use in school settings.

INSTRUCTIONAL CONTENT

We based the content for the *W.A.G.E.S.* curriculum on three sources: (a) The SCANS Report—recommendations from a national committee on the type of skills workers would need to succeed in the workplace in the 21st century (Secretary's Commission on Achieving Necessary Skills, 1991); (b) previous research on the type of social skills needed in the workplace by adolescents with emotional disorders or those judged as at-risk (Bullis & Davis, 1996; Bullis et al., 1993); and (c) ongoing discussions with competitive employers with whom we worked.

The SCANS report. The SCANS (Secretary's Commission on Achieving Necessary Skills) report was developed in conjunction with a select panel of employers and educators to identify the key skills needed by workers to succeed in the workplace in the future. While this panel identified several skill areas, across each area the concept of working well with others, thinking for oneself, and being a "team player" in the workplace was emphasized. These concepts all relate to the concept of job-related social skills—the types of skills we wanted to address, and do address, in the *W.A.G.E.S.* curriculum. **Table 5** identifies those skills areas from the SCANS report and the corresponding lessons in which the *W.A.G.E.S.* curriculum addresses those skills.

Table 5: Comparison of SCANS Competencies and the *W.A.G.E.S.* Curriculum

SCANS COMPETENCIES	W.A.G.E.S. LESSONS AND ACTIVITIES
Basic Skills: Competent individuals in a high-performance workplace need basic skills in reading, writing, arithmetic and mathematics, speaking, and listening.	◄ **Employer Mock Interview & Lessons 21–24** ◄ **RADD Worksheets & Lessons 25–33** ◄ **Pre- & Post-Problem-Solving Vignettes** ◄ **Job Shadow** ◄ **Industry Tour**
Thinking Skills: Competent individuals in a high-performance workplace need the ability to learn, reason, think creatively, make decisions, and solve problems.	◄ **RADD Worksheets & Lessons 25–33** ◄ **Pre- & Post-Problem-Solving Vignettes**
Personal Qualities: Competent individuals in a high-performance workplace need individual responsibility, self-esteem and self-management, sociability, and integrity.	◄ **Communication Lessons 14–24** ◄ **Employer Mock Interview & Lessons 21–24** ◄ **Résumé** ◄ **Letter of Introduction** ◄ **Letter of Appreciation**
Interpersonal Skills: Effective individuals can productively work on teams teaching others, serve customers, lead, negotiate, and work well with people from culturally diverse backgrounds.	◄ **Job Shadow** ◄ **Industry Tour**
Systems: Effective individuals can productively understand social, organizational, and technological systems; they can monitor and correct performance, and can design or improve systems.	◄ **Job Shadow** ◄ **Résumé** ◄ **Cover Letter** ◄ **Letter of Appreciation** ◄ **Employer Mock Interview**

Previous research. For more than a decade we have studied the types of social skills required for adolescents with emotional disorders or who are at-risk to succeed in the work setting (Bullis & Davis, 1996; Bullis et al, 1993). We followed an extensive process of analyzing the work setting from the perspective of adolescents and from the perspective of their employers.

The method we followed is termed the Behavioral Analytic Model (D'Zurilla & Goldfried, 1971), which resulted in a rich and detailed database on the specific types of social interaction problems experienced by adolescents in work settings and the effectiveness of different response alternatives to those interactions. Briefly, that research identified six major areas, or factors, of job-related social skills, from which we chose examples of social interactions on the job to include in the curriculum.

◄ **Factor 1 (Positive Social Behaviors)** consists of skills that relate to general adaptive social behaviors toward work supervisors (e.g., how well does the worker negotiate with the work supervisor to revise or change work tasks?) and coworkers (e.g., how well is the employee able to ask coworkers for assistance to complete a work task?), as well as items related to social skill "mechanics," or the way in which something is said or transmitted (e.g., how well does the worker modulate his or her tone of voice in interactions with the work supervisor?).

◄ **Factor 2 (Negative Social Behaviors)** consists of antisocial behaviors exhibited in the workplace toward work supervisors (e.g., the worker destroys the work supervisor's personal property) or coworkers (e.g., the worker uses profanity when interacting with coworkers), as well as social skills that relate to the individual's ability to resist engaging in antisocial behaviors (e.g., how well is the worker able to resist pressure from coworkers to steal?).

◄ **Factor 3 (Self-Control)** consists of skill in exhibiting self-control toward work supervisors (e.g., the worker has difficulty controlling his or her bad moods in front of the work supervisor) and coworkers (e.g., the worker teases or ridicules coworkers about their appearance or personal habits).

◄ **Factor 4 (Personal Issues)** relates to skill in accepting criticism or correction from the work supervisor (e.g., how well does the worker respond when making a mistake in his or her work?) or addressing an anxiety-provoking subject (e.g., how well does the worker go about talking to the work supervisor about quitting the job?).

◄ **Factor 5 (Body Movements)** relates to controlling body movements in interactions with work supervisors and coworkers.

◄ **Factor 6 (Personal Appearance)** relates to skill in dressing appropriately and maintaining appropriate personal hygiene for the job.

Employer input. During the initial stages of planning and developing the curriculum, we met regularly with employers—owners of businesses and managers of manufacturing plants—to seek their guidance on what skills they thought workers needed to succeed in their particular businesses. Across the group and over time, all stressed the importance of social skills on the job. They stated that they could train workers in how to produce their products, but what they had the most difficulty with was finding workers who would keep a work schedule (i.e., come to work on a regular basis) and interact appropriately with their coworkers and supervisors.

Furthermore, it was clear that a least some of their concern in having workers come to them with these job-related social skills related to retaining their investment. Simply put, if they hired a worker and then trained the individual, there was a sizeable investment in that person—money that would be lost if the worker could not or would not perform in the way in which they were expected on the job.

It was through their input that we decided to emphasize teamwork as a part of the curriculum and attempted to frame the instructional units from the perspective of what employers wanted from their workers.

CURRICULUM FEATURES

Students with behavioral deficits present behaviors that interfere not only with their classroom learning but also with their success in the workplace. Many students with behavioral deficits exhibit poor work environment behaviors. It is well known that students with behavioral deficits lack motivation toward learning new behavioral techniques. Those students do not put forth the effort necessary to learn new, more appropriate, behavioral skills. Furthermore, students who have done poorly in previous work environment curricula fail to utilize formerly learned skills. Moreover, if good workplace behaviors were poorly learned, the expected behaviors may have been used incorrectly or inaccurately, which may have caused negative consequences in a workplace setting. The idea being that, if students do not have a reasonable understanding of applicability of workplace behaviors, they may not know when to utilize them. Thus, *W.A.G.E.S.* was designed as a powerful intervention to ensure that students understand the necessary workplace behaviors, develop reasonable competence in the behaviors, and grasp the applicability of the behaviors.

The *W.A.G.E.S.* curriculum is based upon two features that educational research has shown to be effective (Carnine, 1995). The first is developing multiple interventions that are more understandable and memorable to students with behavioral deficits. The focus is on developing an integrated and comprehensive service-delivery model that utilizes easy-to-understand formats. Importantly, *W.A.G.E.S.* recognizes that workplace behaviors do not consist of a single rule or procedure but are, in fact, combinations of rules and procedures. The *W.A.G.E.S.* strategy is to teach those rules and procedures in combination so that students can develop positive, effective workplace behaviors.

The second curriculum feature is the development of interventions that focus on teaching students the necessary skills and strategies to enable them to successfully negotiate the demands of the workplace environment. Each strategy was created as a set of steps that leads to solving a particular workplace problem. The steps within the *W.A.G.E.S.* curriculum that help students learn include: (a) advance organizers, which provide students with a mental scaffolding; (b) content organization that directs students to assess their own understanding; (c) elaboration, which connects new material to information already learned; and (d) assessment of knowledge, through classroom-based testing or workplace observations. The *W.A.G.E.S.* curriculum organizes the content to create frameworks for understanding the structure of presented content that helps students understand how the information fits together within the curriculum.

EFFECTIVE TEACHING BEHAVIOR

In addition to its curricular features, *W.A.G.E.S.* stresses well-known and effective teaching behaviors: time management, structured content coverage, and feedback (Harris, 1998). A positive relationship between time spent learning and higher student achievement has been found consistently in the research (Dunkin & Biddle, 1974; Kyriacou, 1991; Rosenshine, 1983). Studies have also reinforced the importance of structuring subject content through clear presentation, providing feedback, and effective questioning (Bennett, 1988; Clark & Peterson, 1986; Wittrock, 1986). The *W.A.G.E.S.* curriculum promotes effective teaching by:

◄ Explaining to students what they are to learn. At the start of each lesson, students are told what they will be learning in the day's lesson, thus building a connection to their prior knowledge base and signaling transitions between lesson parts. Also, the main point of the lesson is reviewed at the end of the lesson so that students more easily understand the lesson concept as a whole rather than as a series of isolated skills.

◄ Emphasizing engaged time. Because of the activities built into the lessons, students are on-task a high proportion of the time, and the lessons don't promote socialization and free time.

◄ Providing continuous feedback. During and after each lesson activity, teachers are encouraged to provide feedback on each student's progress towards the expected learning outcome, which helps students make adjustments in their own learning.

◄ Using activities of appropriate difficulty. *W.A.G.E.S.* lessons are suited to the achievement levels and needs of the students being taught.

◄ Accentuating active teaching. In *W.A.G.E.S.* the teachers spend most of their academic time actively (or interactively) teaching rather than students working on their own without guidance; however, the curriculum is not so prescriptive that teachers cannot modify/change the lessons as the class proceeds.

To augment the suggested teaching behaviors, *W.A.G.E.S.* presents information in an approach that emphasizes data organizing, concept understanding, and solution generations. The lessons teach students the importance of working together by taking advantage of the cooperative relationships found in classrooms. Through the lessons, students come to understand themselves better, learn to take responsibility for their own behavioral development, and become increasingly self-aware and responsible for their own behavior.

EFFECTIVE AND PRACTICAL STRUCTURE

We received two federal grants to develop, evaluate, and refine effective secondary curricula for adolescents with emotional disorders and those judged at-risk in order to foster job placement, retention, and advancement toward family-wage jobs (Benz & Bullis, 1998; Bullis & Benz, 1996). Within the umbrella of these grants, we developed the *W.A.G.E.S.* curriculum in conjunction with the Springfield, Oregon, public schools. After extensive discussions with school staff and employers, we decided to adopt the following principles to guide our preliminary development work:

◄ The curriculum should be prepared for delivery in a classroom setting (with 25 to 35 students) by one teacher and one aide and in such a way that it could be sustained and operated by school personnel without benefit of external grant dollars.

◄ The curriculum should be of a length so that it could be delivered in about half a semester (around 9 weeks).

◄ The curriculum should address "real life" social interactions in competitive work settings.

◄ Although the curriculum would focus on adolescents with disabilities, the instruction should be offered in an integrated classroom with typical students.

◄ The instructional approach would be based on the social problem-solving model of behavior and on the elements of "good" instruction.

◄ The curriculum would utilize curriculum-based measurement probes and "authentic" assessments of job-related social skills.

And the *W.A.G.E.S.* curriculum was born. As we developed the curriculum, we conducted multiple studies to be sure that teachers and students liked the curriculum—revising those sections that they said were weak or in need of change—and documented the impact of the instruction on the students (Bullis, Benz, Johnson, & Hollenbeck, 2002). Briefly, we found the following:

◄ Students told us that they enjoyed the curriculum and that they believed the skills they were taught would be important to them.

◄ Average students—those without disabilities—felt that the curriculum was best suited to them at earlier grades—in late middle school or in the freshman year of high school.

◄ Students at-risk and those with disabilities would probably benefit from having the instruction repeated as they gain a new appreciation for the content of the curriculum through supervised work placements, which are often offered later in high school.

◄ Teachers found the curriculum to be clearly organized and useable and liked the "flow" of the lessons.

◄ As indicated by their performance on the curriculum-based measurements within the instructional units, all students improved in their knowledge of job-related social skills from the beginning to the end of each unit. Typical students did tend to score slightly higher than at-risk and disabled students, but these differences were not statistically significant.

◄ Typical, at-risk, and disabled students performed roughly the same on the problem-solving measures in the curriculum, a finding that suggests the power of the curriculum to teach diverse students these important skills.

◄ Evaluations completed by competitive employers who didn't know whether students were disabled, at-risk, or not disabled indicated that all three groups of students performed in similar ways on ratings of their job interview skills.

In sum, these findings provide support for the *W.A.G.E.S.* curriculum as a useable, practical program in any school setting and for the power of the curriculum to teach job-related social skills to diverse groups of students.

We hope that *W.A.G.E.S.* will help your students become productive—and happy—members of the working world!

References

Ager, C., & Cole, C. (1991). A review of cognitive-behavioral interventions for children and adolescents with behavioral disorders. *Behavioral Disorders, 16*, 276–287.

Bandura, A. (1986). *Social foundations of thought and action: A social cognitive theory.* Englewood Cliffs, NJ: Prentice-Hall.

Bennett, N. (1988). The effective primary school teacher: The search for a theory of pedagogy. *Teaching and Teacher Education, 4*, 19–30.

Benz, M., & Bullis, M. (1998). *Secondary school services for adolescents with disabilities: Extending the high school/high skill project.* Washington, DC: Office of Special Education Programs, Model Demonstration Competition, Transition Category.

Benz, M., & Kochhar, C. (1996). School-to-work opportunities for all students: A position statement of the Division on Career Development and Transition. *Career Development for Exceptional Individuals, 19*, 31–48.

Benz, M. R., & Lindstrom, L. E. (1997). *Building school-to-work programs: Strategies for youth with special needs.* Austin, TX: PRO-ED.

Benz, M. R., Yovanoff, P., & Doren, B. (1997). School-to-work components that predict postschool success for students with and without disabilities. *Exceptional Children, 63*, 151–166.

Blackorby, J., & Wagner, M. (1996). Longitudinal postschool outcomes of youth with disabilities: Findings from the National Longitudinal Transition Study. *Exceptional Children, 62*, 399–414.

Bullis, M., & Benz, M. (1996). *Effective secondary/transition programs for adolescents with serious emotional disturbances: The high school/high skill project.* Washington, DC: Office of Special Education Programs, Directed Competition on Effective Secondary Programs for Adolescents with Serious Emotional Disturbance.

Bullis, M., Benz, M., Johnson, M., & Hollenbeck, K. (2002). *Effective secondary/transition programs for adolescents with serious emotional disturbances: The high school/high skill project: Final project report.* Eugene, OR: Institute on Violence and Destructive Behavior, University of Oregon.

Bullis, M., & Davis, C. (1996). Further examination of job-related social skills measures for adolescents and young adults with emotional and behavioral disorders. *Behavioral Disorders, 21*, 161–172.

Bullis, M., & Fredericks, H. D. (Eds.). (2002). *Providing effective vocational/transition services to adolescents with emotional and behavioral disorders.* Champaign-Urbana, IL: Research Press.

Bullis, M., Fredericks, H. D., Lehman, C., Paris, K., Corbitt, J., & Johnson, B. (1994). Description and evaluation of the Job Designs program for adolescents with emotional or behavioral disorders. *Behavioral Disorders, 19*, 254–268.

Bullis, M., Nishioka-Evans, V., Fredericks, H. D., & Davis, C. (1993). Identifying and assessing the job-related social skills of adolescents and young adults with emotional and behavioral disorders. *Journal of Emotional and Behavioral Disorders, 1*, 236–250.

Bullis, M., Tehan, C., & Clark, H. B. (2000). Teaching and developing improved community life competencies. In H. B. Clark & M. Davis (Eds.), *Transition of youth and young adults with emotional/behavioral disturbances into adulthood: Handbook for practitioners, parents, and policymakers* (pp. 107–132). Baltimore: Paul H. Brookes.

Bullis, M., Walker, H., & Sprague, J. (2001). A promise unfulfilled: Social skill training with at-risk and antisocial children and youth. *Exceptionality, (1 & 2)*, 69–92.

Bullis, M., & Yovanoff, P. (2002). *The importance of getting started right: Examination of the community engagement of formerly incarcerated youth.* Manuscript submitted for publication, Eugene, OR: University of Oregon, College of Education, Institute on Violence and Destructive behavior.

Bullis, M., Yovanoff, P, Mueller, G., & Havel, E. (in press). Life on the "outs": Examination of the facility-to-community transition of incarcerated adolescents. *Exceptional Children.*

Carnine, D. (1995). Trustworthiness, usability, and accessibility of educational research. *Journal of Behavioral Education, 5*, 251–258.

Chadsey-Rusch, J. (1990). Teaching social skills on the job. In F. Rusch (Ed.), *Supported employment: Models, methods, and issues* (pp. 161–180). Sycamore, IL: Sycamore.

Chandler, M. (1973). Egocentricism and antisocial behavior: The assessment and training of social perspective skills. *Developmental Psychology, 9*, 326–332.

Clark, C. M., & Peterson, P. L. (1986). Teachers thought processes. In M. Wittrock (Ed.), *Handbook of research teaching (3rd Ed).* New York: Macmillan.

Cook, J. A., Solomon, M. L., & Mock, L. O. (1988). *What happens after the first job placement: Vocational transitioning among severely emotionally disturbed and behavior disordered adolescents.* Chicago: Thresholds Research Institute.

Crites, J. (1989). Career development in adolescence: Theory, measurement, and longitudinal findings. In D. Stern & D. Eichorn (Eds.), *Adolescence and work: Influences of social structure, labor markets, and culture* (pp. 141–158). Hillsdale, NJ: Lawrence Earlbaum.

Dishion, T. J., Loeber, R., Stouthamer-Loeber, M., & Patterson, G. (1984). Skills deficits and male adolescent delinquency. *Journal of Abnormal Child Psychology, 12,* 37–54.

Dodge, K. (1980). Social cognition and children's aggressive behavior. *Child Development, 51,* 162–170.

Dodge, K., & Frame, C. (1980). Social cognitive biases and deficits in aggressive boys. *Child Development, 53,* 620–635.

Dodge, K., & Newman, J. (1981). Biased decision-making processes in aggressive boys. *Journal of Abnormal Psychology, 90,* 375–450.

Dodge, K., Price, J., Bachorowski, J., & Newman, J. (1990). Hostile attributional biases in severely aggressive adolescents. *Journal of Abnormal Psychology, 99,* 385–392.

Donovan, J., & Jessor, R. (1985). Structure of problem behavior in adolescence and young adulthood. *Journal of Consulting and Clinical Psychology, 53,* 890–904.

Dunkin, M. J., & Biddle, B. J. (1974). *The study of teaching.* New York: Holt, Rinehart, and Winston.

D'Zurilla, T. J. (1986). *Problem solving therapy: A social competence approach to clinical intervention.* New York: Springer.

D'Zurilla, T., & Goldfried, M. (1971). Problem solving and behavior modification. *Journal of Abnormal Psychology, 78,* 107–126.

Eisenberg, N., & Miller, P. (1987). The relation of empathy to pro-social and related behaviors. *Psychological Bulletin, 101,* 91–119.

Eisenberg, N., & Strayer, J. (Eds.). (1987). *Empathy and its development.* Cambridge: Cambridge University Press.

Freedman, B. J., Rosenthal, L., Donahoe, C. P., Schlundt, D. G., & McFall, R. M. (1978). A social-behavioral analysis of skill deficits in delinquent and nondelinquent boys. *Journal of Consulting and Clinical Psychology, 46,* 1448–1462.

Gaffney, L. (1984). A multiple-choice test to measure social skills in delinquent and nondelinquent adolescent girls. *Journal of Consulting and Clinical Psychology, 52,* 911–912.

Gaffney, L. R., & McFall, R. M. (1981). A comparison of social skills in delinquent and nondelinquent adolescent girls using a behavioral role-playing inventory. *Journal of Consulting and Clinical Psychology, 49,* 959–967.

Gresham, F. (1997). Social competence and students with behavior disorders: Where we've been, where we are, and where we should go. *Education and Treatment of Children, 20,* 233–249.

Gresham, F. (1998). Social skills training: Should we raze, remodel, or rebuild? *Behavioral Disorders, 24,* 19–25.

Griffiths, R. (1974). Rehabilitation of chronic psychiatric patients. *Psychological Medicine, 4,* 311–325.

Harris, A. (1998). Effective teaching: A review of the literature. *School Leadership and Management, 18,* 169–184.

Hasazi, S. B., Gordon, L. R., & Roe, C. (1985). Factors associated with the employment status of handicapped youth exiting high school from 1979 to 1983. *Exceptional Children, 51,* 455–469.

Henderson, M., & Hollin, C. (1983). A critical review of social skills training with young offenders. *Criminal Justice and Behavior, 10,* 316–341.

Henggler, S. (1989). *Delinquency in adolescence.* Beverly Hills, CA: Sage.

Kazdin, A. (1979). Situational specificity: The two-edged sword of behavioral assessment. *Behavioral Assessment, 1,* 57–59.

Kazdin, A. (1987). *Conduct disorders in childhood and adolescence.* Beverly Hills, CA: Sage.

Kohler, P. (1993). Best practices in transition: Substantiated or implied? *Career Development for Exceptional Individuals, 16,* 107–121.

Kyriacou, C. (1991). *Essential teaching skills.* Oxford: Basil Blackwell.

Lochman, J. (1992). Cognitive-behavioral intervention with aggressive boys: Three-year follow-up and preventive effects. *Journal of Consulting and Clinical Psychology, 60,* 426–432.

Marzillier, J. (1980). Cognitive therapy and behavioral practice. *Behavior Research and Therapy, 18,* 249–258.

McFall, R. (1982). A review and reformulation of the concept of social skills. *Behavioral Assessment, 4,* 1–33.

Meichenbaum, D. (1977). *Cognitive-behavior modification.* New York: Plenum Press.

Meyers, A., & Cohen, R. (1990). Cognitive-behavioral approaches to child psychopathology: Present status and future directions. In M. Lewis & S. Miller (Eds.), *Handbook of developmental psychopathology* (pp. 475–485). New York: John Wiley & Sons.

Nishioka, V., & Bullis, M. (2002). Job-related social skills training. In M. Bullis & H. D. Fredericks (Eds.), *Providing effective vocational/transition services to adolescents with emotional and behavioral disorders* (pp. 133–152). Champaign-Urbana, IL: Research Press.

Osipow, S. (1983). *Theory of career development (3rd ed.).* Englewood Cliffs, NJ: Prentice Hall.

Parker, J., & Asher, S. (1987). Peer relations and later personal adjustment: Are low-accepted children at risk? *Psychological Bulletin, 102,* 357–389.

Platt, J. J., Spivack, G., Altman, N., Altman, D., & Seizer, S. B. (1974). Adolescent problem-solving thinking. *Journal of Consulting and Clinical Psychology, 42,* 787–793.

Rosenshine, B. (1983). Teaching functions in instructional programs. *Elementary School Journal, 83,* 335–351.

Rusch, F. (1995). Reflections: Ten years of the Transition Research Institute. *Interchange, 13*(4), 1–2.

Sacks, S. Z., Tierney-Russell, D., Hirsch, M., & Braden, J. (1992). Social skills training: What professionals say they do. In S. Z. Sacks, D. Tierney-Russell, M. Hirsch, & J. Braden (Eds.), *The status of social skills training in special education and rehabilitation: Present and future trends.* Nashville, TN: Vanderbilt University.

Schumaker, J., Pederson, C. S., Hazel, J. S. & Meyen, E. L. (1983). Social skills curricula for mildly handicapped adolescents: A review. *Focus on Exceptional Children, 16*(4), 1–16.

Shamise, S. (1981). Antisocial adolescents: Our treatments do not work—Where do we go from here? *Canadian Journal of Psychiatry, 26,* 357–364.

Sitlington, P., Frank, A., & Carson, R. (1992). Adult adjustment among high school graduates with mild disabilities. *Exceptional Children, 59,* 221–233.

Spence, S. (1981a). Validation of social skills of adolescent males in an interview conversation with a previously unknown adult. *Journal of Applied Behavior Analysis, 14,* 159–168.

Spence, S. (1981b). Differences in social skills performance between institutionalized juvenile male offenders and a comparable group of boys without offense records. *British Journal of Clinical Psychology, 20,* 163–171.

The Secretary's Commission on Achieving Necessary Skills. (1991). *What work requires of schools: A SCANS report for America 2000.* Washington, DC: U.S. Dept. of Labor.

Urbain, E., & Kendall, P. (1980). Review of social-cognitive problem solving interventions with children. *Psychological Bulletin, 88,* 109–143.

Wagner, M. (1992). Analytic overview: NLTS design and longitudinal analysis approach. In M. Wagner, R. D'Amico, C. Marder, L. Newman, & J. Blackorby (Eds.), *Trends in postschool outcomes of youth with disabilities* (pp. 2-1 to 2-14). Menlo Park, CA: SRI International.

Will, M. (1984). *OSERS program for the transition of youth with disabilities: Bridges from school to working life.* Washington, DC: U.S. Dept. Of Education, Office of Special Education and Rehabilitative Services.

Wittrock, M. (1986). *Handbook of research on teaching (3rd ed).* New York: Macmillan.

PART TWO

UNIT 1

LESSONS 1–2

INTRODUCTION

LESSON 1

Getting the Ball Rolling

PURPOSE:	**THIS LESSON PROVIDES AN INTRODUCTION TO WORKPLACE SOCIAL SKILLS AND TO THE CURRICULUM IN GENERAL.**
	Utilizing a panel of 4–5 community patrons who work in various career fields, students will gain an appreciation for those workplace foundation skills and attitudes that are necessary to survive and succeed on the job.
PRE-LESSON ACTIVITY— CURRICULUM- BASED MEASUREMENT (10 MINUTES)	**HAND OUT THE CBM VOCABULARY TEST #1** (SEE APPENDIX) **TO THE STUDENTS.** Time them for seven minutes, then collect their tests. Be sure to administer the test *before* beginning this lesson. You will use the CBM results as a guide to student progress on vocabulary concepts.
LEARNING OUTCOMES	◄ Students will be able to identify several workplace social skills and attitudes that are valued by employers.
REQUIRED MATERIALS	◄ Flip chart or white board/chalkboard ◄ Panel Questionnaire ◄ CBM Vocabulary Test #1
LESSON 1 VOCABULARY	**DISTRIBUTE THE UNIT ONE VOCABULARY LIST.** **HAVE STUDENTS REFER TO THE UNIT ONE VOCABULARY LIST AS YOU INTRODUCE THE FOLLOWING VOCABULARY WORDS.** **Workplace Social Skills:** Those social interaction skills that are necessary for a person to succeed in gaining and maintaining employment.

DESCRIPTION OF ACTIVITY

Activity 1.1   "What Will Employers Expect Of Me?" (40 MINUTES)

This activity will allow students to generate a list of workplace qualities that are valued in various career fields and work environments. A panel of 4–5 community patrons representing diverse career options (e.g., fast food worker, police officer, electrician, business leader) will respond to questions and provide insight on what it takes to succeed on the job. Assemble the patrons through school contacts or through your school's parent-teacher group.

◄ Provide students and panel members with the **questionnaire** that will be used to stimulate discussion around workplace social skills and attitudes.

◄ Students should **record** the responses of the panel to each item on the questionnaire.

◄ After the panel discussion has concluded, have students compile a **cumulative list** of desirable workplace social skills and attitudes on a flip chart or whiteboard/chalkboard.

◄ Make letter-sized copies of the compiled skills list for use in Lesson 2.

WRAP-UP/HOMEWORK

Explain to the students that they will be playing the "Making *W.A.G.E.S.* Contest," a fun question-and-answer team game, in the next lesson. During that lesson they will learn how those workplace qualities addressed by the panel will be transformed into a game that relates to the entire course structure. They should realize that today's lesson answered the question of what qualities are most valued by employers but that the next lesson will provide an enjoyable structure for learning more about those qualities.

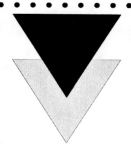

Panel Questionnaire

1. Would each of you please identify yourselves by name and tell us a little about where you work and what you do?

2. What are some of the jobs that you have held in your lifetime that clearly stand out in your memory? Why?

3. What sorts of things are employers looking for when they hire a new employee?

4. What are the reasons that employees lose their jobs?

5. Can you provide us with some examples of how employees demonstrated the qualities described in the last two questions?

6. What sorts of things can students be doing right now to prepare themselves to succeed in the workplace?

7. Student questions?

LESSON 2

W.A.G.E.S. Program Overview

PURPOSE	**THIS LESSON IS AN OPPORTUNITY FOR STUDENTS TO UNDERSTAND THE SCOPE AND SEQUENCE OF THE COURSE.** Through the lesson, students will become familiar with the foundation skills and attitudes associated with being a successful worker. The "Making *W.A.G.E.S.* Contest" provides a forum for students to become familiar with vocabulary and content pertinent to later lessons and activities in the curriculum.
LEARNING OUTCOMES	◄ Students will demonstrate knowledge of the four foundation skills (i.e., locus of control, teamwork, communication, problem solving) necessary to make successful connections on the job. ◄ Students will demonstrate knowledge of the attitudes (e.g., dependability, honesty, enthusiasm) associated with effective social skills on the job.
REVIEW	Explain to students that the qualities for workplace success that were generated in Lesson 1 will be the basis for teaching the remainder of the course. Have them refer to their workplace-qualities list as they learn more in Lesson 2 of how these skills will be taught.
REQUIRED MATERIALS	◄ Overheads (2) on *W.A.G.E.S.* Foundation Skills and Attitudes ◄ Flip chart or white board/chalkboard ◄ "Making *W.A.G.E.S.*" game cards (see Appendix) ◄ "Making *W.A.G.E.S.*" Tally Sheet ◄ Timer or clock ◄ Treats or some other incentive List of workplace qualities (GENERATED IN LESSON 1)

LESSON 2
VOCABULARY

FOUNDATION SKILLS: Those social skills or attitudes that are most important for experiencing success on the job. Foundation skills include:

Locus of Control (LOC): The "location" of an individual's sense of personal control or responsibility over actions and events. Example: People who tend to blame others have a locus of control that is located outside of themselves.

◀ **Internal Locus of Control:** "Internal locus of control" is a measure that determines how much self-control and responsibility a person has for his or her own behavior. People with a strong internal locus of control tend to "own," or take credit or blame for, their actions. Example: apologizing for being late to a meeting without making excuses.

◀ **External Locus of Control:** "External locus of control" is a measure of how little self-control and responsibility a person has for his or her own behavior. People with a strong external locus of control tend to "moan" about, or place credit or blame for, their actions on events or people outside of their own control. Example: whining or making excuses about being late to a meeting.

Teamwork: The measure of a person's ability to work with others to accomplish a task. Example: a group of workers efficiently moving furniture into a home.

Communication: The measure of how well a person makes his or her thoughts and feelings known to others. Example: maintaining good eye contact with your employer while discussing work tasks.

Problem Solving: The measure of how well a person can develop strategies for overcoming obstacles or issues with people or situations. Example: figuring out how to ask your boss for more hours on the job.

ATTITUDES: Those qualities that a person needs to reflect a positive attitude on the job. They include:

Dependability: The measure of how much a person can be relied upon by coworkers and supervisors to perform work-related tasks. Example: showing up on time ready to work every day.

Honesty: The measure of how much a person is truthful to and respectful of coworkers and supervisors. Example: confessing about losing a tool that was important to all workers in the shop.

Enthusiasm: The measure of how much a person enjoys his or her work and expresses that enjoyment appropriately to others. Example: encouraging coworkers to eat lunch together once a week.

DESCRIPTION OF ACTIVITY

ACTIVITY 2.1　**OVERVIEW OF CURRICULUM** (10 MINUTES)

This activity will allow students to take the list of ideas that was generated in Lesson 1 and tie those qualities, skills, attitudes, etc., into the scope and sequence of the curriculum.

◀ **Post** the list of desired workplace qualities that the students generated during Activity 1.1 in Lesson 1, or **copy** the list and make a handout available to each student.

◀ Using the **Foundation Skills and Attitudes overheads**, provide students with the big picture overview of the entire course. Explain the definitions of each of the vocabulary words on these overheads to the students (you will need to give the students definitions for vocabulary words in each of the lessons as you progress through the curriculum). Refer to their list of desirable workplace qualities as the units of instruction are discussed, explaining that those workplace qualities they generated will be taught within the four units of "Locus of Control," "Teamwork," "Communication," and "Problem Solving." Attempt to get students excited about the course by explaining that they will be doing many enjoyable, hands-on activities. Also, let them know that rewards/incentives will be used periodically.

◀ **Write** the four foundation skills (the names of the four units) that represent the scope and sequence of the curriculum on the board or flip chart.

◀ **Task:** Attempt to categorize all of the student-generated responses from their desirable workplace qualities list under the four foundation skills. Explain that the social skills that have been discussed can be recorded within each of the four foundation skill areas. For example, the students might have generated "cooperation" as a desirable workplace quality. This might be categorized under both "Teamwork" and "Problem Solving."

ACTIVITY 2.2　**"MAKING *W.A.G.E.S.* CONTEST"** (30 MINUTES)

This activity will introduce students to a game where they can compete for incentives by demonstrating their level of knowledge of course content. The game can be repeated occasionally to review vocabulary and concepts contained within the curriculum. Students should be able to demonstrate higher levels of learning and performance as the game is repeated.

◀ **Divide** students into a maximum of three teams. Provide each team with a "Making *W.A.G.E.S.*" Tally Sheet that reflects the four content areas to be addressed in the course. A reproducible master of the tally sheet is included later in this lesson.

◀ **Explain** to students that they will be asked to define or perform certain tasks contained on the back of the "Making *W.A.G.E.S.*" cards in each of the four content areas; tasks are worth from 100 to 500 points. Tell them that "the higher the number of points, the more difficult the problem." When playing the game for the first time, it is advisable to limit game cards to 100- and 200-point questions. As teams choose cards and correctly answer the problems presented on the back of each card, members will keep track of points scored with each round played. It is a good idea for you to keep track of the points on the board or overhead as well. In addition, you will need to judge students' performance on some of the questions to determine if they earned the points.

◀ **Requirements:** Each team will be given two minutes to solve as many problems as possible without making a mistake. During the two-minute round, each team member must take a turn selecting a problem of varying point value and provide a reasonable answer to the teacher in order to score points. The problems chosen by team members must be representative of all four foundation skills (Locus of Control; Teamwork; Communication; Problem Solving). In other words, members must select a problem from within each of the four areas before repeating a category; for example, a second problem from Teamwork cannot be selected before problems from the other three categories are chosen. Team members may only ask for assistance from teammates in situations where the answer requires a role-play scenario.

◀ The **Object** of the game is for teams to score the highest number of points in the total amount of time available. **Hint:** Choosing to answer easier questions for fewer points may mean a better chance of earning team points, but risking harder problems will generate more points per question for a team. At the end of play, total points earned throughout the game determine the winner. Incentives for the winners should be given (e.g., free time, treats, etc.).

WRAP-UP/HOMEWORK

As students play the "Making *W.A.G.E.S.*" contest, they will progressively become more capable of performing tasks and answering questions of higher value. The lessons that follow will focus more specifically on each of the content areas highlighted by the game. Explain to students that they will have a better chance of responding to cards with higher values as they participate in the next lessons in the curriculum.

Team Name _____

Making *W.A.G.E.S.*
Tally Sheet

LOCUS OF CONTROL	TEAMWORK	COMMUNICATION	PROBLEM SOLVING
TOTAL:	**TOTAL:**	**TOTAL:**	**TOTAL:**

GRAND TOTAL:_____

W.A.G.E.S.

FOUNDATION SKILLS

☑ **LOCUS OF CONTROL**

☑ **TEAMWORK**

☑ **COMMUNICATION**

☑ **PROBLEM SOLVING**

W.A.G.E.S.

ATTITUDES

 **ENTHUSIASM**

 **DEPENDABILITY**

 **HONESTY**

UNIT
2

LESSONS 3–8

LOCUS OF CONTROL

LESSON 3

Locus of Control = RESPONSIBILITY

PURPOSE	THIS LESSON PROVIDES AN OPPORTUNITY FOR STUDENTS TO UNDERSTAND WHAT IT MEANS TO TAKE RESPONSIBILITY FOR THEIR OWN ACTIONS.
	Students will learn how to differentiate between an internal and an external locus of control (LOC). This lesson will emphasize the value of an internal locus of control in job settings.
COMPLEMENTARY ACTIVITIES	At some point during Unit Two, schedule a day for the career guidance activity suggested in **Table 3** of the Instructor's Guide.
LEARNING OUTCOMES	◀ Students will understand that LOC is a framework for measuring their ownership (responsibility) of a situation or problem. ◀ Students will understand that LOC can be reflected in actions or words that are external or internal. ◀ Students will recognize behaviors that suggest a person is acting in an internal manner (taking responsibility) or an external manner (not taking responsibility) by the person's actions or reactions.
REQUIRED MATERIALS	◀ Newspaper articles that exemplify internal and external LOC ◀ Locus of Control Worksheet ◀ Locus of Control Log for homework
LESSON 3 VOCABULARY	REFER TO THE UNIT TWO VOCABULARY LIST AS YOU REVIEW THE FOLLOWING VOCABULARY PHRASES. **Locus of Control (LOC):** The "location" of an individual's sense of personal control or responsibility over actions and events. For example, people who tend to blame others have a locus of control that is located outside of themselves. **Internal Locus of Control:** "Internal locus of control" is a measure that determines how much self-control and responsibility a person has for his or her own behavior. People with a strong internal locus of control tend to "own," or take credit or blame for, their actions. Example: apologizing for being late to a meeting without making excuses. **External Locus of Control:** "External locus of control" is a measure of how little self-control and responsibility a person has for his or her own behavior. People with a strong external locus of control tend to "moan" about, or place credit or blame for, their actions. Example: whining or making excuses about being late.

DESCRIPTION OF ACTIVITY:

ACTIVITY 3.1 **NEWSPAPER ARTICLE** (25 MINUTES)

THIS ACTIVITY WILL ALLOW STUDENTS TO RECOGNIZE REAL-LIFE SITUATIONS INVOLVING AN INTERNAL AND AN EXTERNAL LOCUS OF CONTROL.

◄ Introduce the lesson by reading an article from the local newspaper that demonstrates that the person being described in the story has little sense of personal responsibility (e.g., suing a gun manufacturer for making the weapon that killed someone's child). Discuss this person's locus of control with the students.

◄ Ask students if they can think of other people and situations where a sense of self-control was lacking (e.g., hallways at break, lunchroom, athletic contest).

◄ Read an article that demonstrates or shows a person with a high level of personal responsibility. Discuss this person's degree of self-control with the students.

◄ Have students think of other people and situations where self-control was demonstrated (e.g., raising hand vs. interrupting, handing the ball to a referee after a bad call vs. yelling at him, staying "cool" after missing a putt vs. throwing your club). Emphasize the importance of self-control.

◄ Explain that behaviors or statements that demonstrate a lack of control or ownership tend to be "external" in nature. Conversely, behaviors and statements that exemplify self-control and ownership can be viewed as "internal."

Have students provide examples of statements that demonstrate internal or external locus of control. List their ideas on a flip chart or board under **"Moaning/Placing Blame or Credit/External"** or **"Owning/Taking Blame or Credit/Internal."** Explain that you want to be sure they understand the difference between an internal and an external locus of control, as it is important to practice "owning" your own behaviors. They might give an example such as, "My alarm didn't go off. That's why I was late." They then should be able to identify this as **"Moaning/Placing Blame or Credit/External."**

ACTIVITY 3.2: **LOC WORKSHEET** (15 MINUTES)

THIS ACTIVITY WILL ALLOW STUDENTS TO DEMONSTRATE IN WRITING THEIR UNDERSTANDING OF THE DIFFERENCE BETWEEN AN INTERNAL AND AN EXTERNAL LOCUS OF CONTROL.

◄ Hand out the LOC Worksheet to all students.

◄ Model the first item so that they get the idea of how to write an internal or external locus response to a statement or situation. Prompt the students for ideas of how to complete the first item. Basically, they are to write an internal and external response to each statement.

◄ Give students 10–15 minutes to complete the worksheet individually. Students may talk to one another while working on the assignment. (As a time-saving alternative, you may give this worksheet as homework to be done before the next lesson.)

WRAP-UP/HOMEWORK: (5 MINUTES)

Hand out the LOC Log sheet to each student. Explain that this sheet will be assigned as ongoing homework during the four units of the course. We suggest that you make the first completed log sheet due within two to three days. Four more completed log sheets should be due at various times throughout the remainder of the course (for example, every fifth class meeting). Walk students through some examples of how they will record events that occur that reflect internal and external locus of control. It is helpful to reward students for log entries as they continue to participate in remaining lessons. If grades are used, five complete logs over the course of the term or semester could be equated with an "A," four could be a "B," and so on.

Locus of Control Worksheet

Directions: Provide a possible internal response and a possible external response for each situation.

1. Martin got an "F" on his science test. When the teacher asked him about it, he replied: (Example for internal: "I need to study harder.")

Internal   **External**

2. Teresa was drinking a can of soda. She left it on top of the computer, even though her boss asked her to remove it. When a coworker knocked it over, the computer short-circuited. When her boss asked her about it, she said:

Internal   **External**

3. Bruce wanted to get out of doing some work, so he told the boss that he had almost finished the job and then he asked for a break. Later, his boss found out that Bruce hadn't even started the job and confronted him. Bruce said:

Internal   **External**

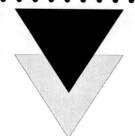

Name:_____

Locus of Control Log
Did you OWN or MOAN?

Directions: Give an example of when you used either an internal or external locus of control while you were at work, school, or some other place (preferably a work situation). Describe the situation, then decide if you showed an internal or external locus of control. Explain why you think this situation represents an internal or external locus of control.

FOR WEEK OF:

DAY	EVENT/SITUATION	EXTERNAL OR INTERNAL? EXPLAIN. . .

Lesson 4

What Does "Locus of Control" Mean to the Team? (Part One)

Purpose	**In this lesson students will participate in an activity that will reinforce their understanding of an internal and external locus of control.**
	They will identify and exemplify various situations or behaviors reflecting internal vs. external locus of control. This lesson provides one of the first opportunities for students to participate in a role-play activity.
Learning Outcomes	◄ Students will continue tracking internal vs. external locus of control in their activity logs.
	◄ Students will work in pairs to identify examples of "owning" vs. "moaning" behaviors.
	◄ Students will demonstrate these behaviors and attitudes through a role-playing activity.
Review (5 minutes)	Ask students to identify and discuss the examples of "owning" or "moaning" attitudes and behaviors from the LOC Worksheet. Have those who are willing volunteer real-life examples of owning vs. moaning from their LOC Logs. Reinforce them for volunteering and call on others if enough do not volunteer.
Required Materials	◄ Scissors
	◄ Locus of Control Examples (to be cut out)
	◄ Locus of Control Log from Lesson 3
	◄ Draw box or hat
Lesson 4 Vocabulary	**Have students refer to their Unit One Vocabulary List as you introduce the following vocabulary word.**
	Role-Play To act out a situation, behavior, or attitude as if it were really happening. Example: "becoming" or acting like an angry student who makes excuses about not doing his or her homework.

DESCRIPTION OF ACTIVITY:

ACTIVITY 4.1   **BE A 'LOCUS OF CONTROL' TEAM** (45 MINUTES)

This activity will allow students to work as a team to earn points related to locus of control knowledge. The students will have the opportunity to role-play situations. Only half of the teams will perform role-plays in this class. The other half of the teams will perform role-plays during the next lesson (Lesson 5).

◄ Have students form teams of 2–3 people and choose a team name. Write the team names on a flip chart or board. Explain that only half of the teams will perform role-plays in this lesson.

◄ Let each team select a statement/scenario from the draw box or hat (you will need to cut scenarios from the Locus of Control Examples sheet). Give the teams about five minutes to communicate about their statements. The team decides whether the statement demonstrates an internal or external locus of control. Each team selects a spokesman who will read the statement aloud and identify the locus of control as either "internal/owning" or "external/moaning."

◄ Each team also will have the option of earning additional points by giving an opposite example (i.e., they will give an internal situation if the situation they drew was external) or by role-playing the situation they drew. The teams will have to be creative in role-playing situations that reflect the statement on the slip, as the statement will be brief, and creative thought will be required to come up with a role-play situation.

◄ If the team opts not to earn additional points, then other teams may earn the extra points by volunteering opposite examples.

◄ Have the entire class evaluate the examples and role-plays. A few examples could potentially be internal or external. It is the team's rationale for their decision that matters most in those situations. You should make the final decision for who does and does not receive points in each situation.

◄ The winner is determined by the team having the most points after everyone has presented (which probably will not be until the end of the next lesson—Lesson 5).

  – **1** point   For identifying whether the statement reflects "internal" or "external."

  – **2** points   For giving an example of the opposite response.

  – **3** points   For acting out the statement or scenario.

Total: **6** points (+ any extra credit points for volunteering examples; we suggest 1 point per extra example or role-play).

◄ Keep a record of the team scores from this lesson in order to compare them to the team scores in the next lesson.

WRAP-UP/HOMEWORK

Hand out another LOC Log sheet to those students who need one. Remind the students that this is homework and that they should do it over the course of the remaining lessons. If necessary, walk them through some more examples of how they will record events that occur that reflect internal and external locus of control. Remember to reward students for log entries as they continue to participate in the remaining lessons.

Locus of Control

Examples of "Owning" or "Moaning"

◀ *"Our team wouldn't have had a chance of winning if I didn't wear my lucky jersey."*

◀ After being accused of working too slowly by your supervisor, you say:

"I'm really doing the best that I can. I must not understand the speed that you want me to work at."

◀ Max has just realized that he has missed a meeting. He will be half an hour late if he tries to get there. Max calls his counselor and says:

"I totally spaced this meeting. Do you still want me to come in?"

◀ Keith was not able to finish his math assignment in time for the due date, and the next day in class says:

"Things have really been crazy around my house; my sister is getting married, and no one could help me with this assignment." (This is a true statement.)

◀ *"My friends pick on me because I am heavier than they are. I can't do anything about it!"*

◀ *"My parents really don't listen to me as much as they do my sister. I should talk to them about this."*

◀ *"The President has really been framed by the Republicans."*

◀ *"I've tried everything with Johnny. He just doesn't care, and neither do I."*

◀ *"I'm not going to answer that question, because I'll look like the teacher's pet."*

Locus of Control
Examples of "Owning" or "Moaning"
(continued)

◀ *"When life gives you lemons, make lemonade . . ."*

◀ *"I'm not going to her party, because I won't know anyone."*

◀ *"I'm fed up with you guys sitting on your fannies while I'm doing your job!"*

◀ *"I can't help it. You never made that clear to me."*

◀ A lawsuit claiming that a gun manufacturer is responsible for an accidental shooting where a child pulled the trigger of a loaded pistol.

◀ *"I could have played much better if I had focused before the game."*

◀ *"Sorry I'm late."*

◀ *"You promised me!"*

◀ *"I'm sorry, but I forgot your name."*

◀ *"Oh, whatever!"*

◀ *"My cup is half full, not half empty"*

◀ *"Why can't I take a long lunch? Everybody else does."*

◀ *"I can't work this weekend, but I would be happy to on any other weekend this month."*

LESSON 5

What Does "Locus of Control" Mean to the Team? (Part Two)

PURPOSE	THIS LESSON IS A CONTINUATION OF LESSON 4 AND ALLOWS STUDENTS TO CONTINUE PARTICIPATION IN AN ACTIVITY THAT REINFORCES THEIR UNDERSTANDING OF AN INTERNAL AND EXTERNAL LOCUS OF CONTROL. The remaining teams will identify and exemplify various situations or behaviors reflecting internal vs. external locus of control. This lesson also provides students with an opportunity to create and role-play familiar scenarios depicting either an internal or an external locus of control.
LEARNING OUTCOMES	◀ Students will continue tracking internal vs. external locus of control in their LOC Logs. ◀ Students will work in pairs to create examples of "owning" vs. "moaning" behaviors. ◀ Students will demonstrate these behaviors and attitudes through a role-playing activity.
REVIEW (5 MINUTES)	Ask for students to volunteer examples from their LOC Logs. Discuss these examples as a class. Reinforce them for volunteering and call on others if enough do not volunteer.
REQUIRED MATERIALS	◀ Scissors ◀ Locus of Control Examples (remaining from Lesson 4) ◀ Locus of Control Blanks (to be written and then cut out) ◀ Locus of Control Log from Lesson 3 ◀ Draw box or hat ◀ CBM Vocabulary Test #2
LESSON 5 VOCABULARY	There is no new vocabulary for this lesson.

DESCRIPTION OF ACTIVITY

ACTIVITY 5.1:   **BE A 'LOCUS OF CONTROL' TEAM** (35 MINUTES)

Students will get back into the same teams from Lesson 4. Allow teams that did not get a chance to finish reacting to their scenarios from the previous day to do so. After each team has had their turn, all teams will generate five new situations that are familiar examples of "owning" or "moaning" attitudes and behaviors.

◄ Have students get back into their teams of 2–3 people and repeat their team name. Write the team names on a flip chart or board. Record the scores from Lesson 4 on the board. Explain that the remaining teams will perform role-plays at the beginning of this lesson.

◄ Have each team use the same statement/scenario they drew during Lesson 4. Give the teams about five minutes to communicate about their statements. The team decides whether the statement demonstrates an internal or external locus of control. Each team selects a spokesman who will read the statement aloud and identify the locus of control as either "internal/owning" or "external/moaning."

◄ Each team also will have the option of earning additional points by giving an opposite example (i.e., they will give an internal situation if the situation they drew was external) and role-playing the situation they drew. The teams will have to be creative in role-playing situations that reflect the statement on the slip, as often the statement will be brief and will require creative thought to form a role-play situation.

◄ If the team opts not to earn additional points, then other teams may earn the extra points by volunteering examples.

◄ Have the entire class evaluate the examples and the role-plays. A few examples could potentially be internal or external. It is the team's rationale for their decision that matters most in those situations. You should make the final decision for who does and does not receive points in each situation.

◄ Using the Locus of Control Blanks, have each team generate five new situations that are familiar examples of "owning" or "moaning" attitudes and behaviors. Start another round of the locus of control game utilizing the newly generated examples of "owning" and "moaning."

◄ The winner is determined by the team having the most points after everyone has presented.

   – **1** point   For identifying whether the statement reflects "internal" or "external."

   – **2** points   For giving an example of the opposite response.

   – **3** points   For acting out the statement or scenario.

Total: **6** points (+ any extra credit points for volunteering examples; we suggest 1 point per extra example or role-play).

CBM (10 MINUTES)

Hand out the CBM Vocabulary Test #2 to the students. Time them for seven minutes, then collect their tests. Use the results as a guide to student progress on vocabulary concepts.

WRAP-UP/HOMEWORK

Discuss the game with your students, asking for feedback from them. Did they enjoy the game? Do they feel they understand LOC more completely now? Explain that the next couple of lessons will also be related to LOC but will focus specifically on self-control.

Locus of Control Blanks

LESSON 6

Self-Control (Part One)

PURPOSE	**THIS LESSON INTRODUCES STUDENTS TO STRATEGIES THAT WILL HELP THEM MAINTAIN SELF-CONTROL IN STRESSFUL SITUATIONS.**
	They will understand how these strategies help people operate from an internal locus of control. Students will investigate what causes them to lose control and how they react emotionally and physically to stress.
LEARNING OUTCOMES	◄ Students will be able to identify common "firecrackers" that cause them to lose self-control.
	◄ Students will use a "pressure gauge" to detect the physical/emotional signals that occur as they begin to lose self-control.
REVIEW (5 MINUTES)	Ask students for examples of people who have lost control under stress. Explain that these are the behaviors that cost people relationships and jobs. As they talk about these events or situations attempt to help students understand the connection between locus of control and self-control. Affirm that acting from an internal locus of control encourages people to demonstrate a higher level of self-control.
REQUIRED MATERIALS	◄ Flip chart or white board
	◄ "I'm Going Off!" Worksheet
LESSON 6 VOCABULARY	**HAVE STUDENTS REFER TO THEIR UNIT ONE VOCABULARY LIST AS YOU INTRODUCE THE FOLLOWING VOCABULARY WORDS.**
	Firecracker: A word, statement, or action that makes a person "go off" and begin to lose self-control. Example: being called "stupid" by a coworker when you ask an honest question.
	Pressure Gauge: The physical/emotional indicator that signifies someone is under stress and losing control. For example, sweaty palms, clenched fists, a red face, a tight stomach, elevated breathing, and a suffocating feeling are all indicators of starting to lose self-control.

DESCRIPTION OF ACTIVITY

ACTIVITY 6.1 **"I'M GOING OFF!"** (20 MINUTES)

This activity allows students the opportunity to identify common "firecrackers" that set them off. They will also become familiar with their personal "pressure gauge," which registers stress and a loss of control.

◄ **Discuss** what sets people "off" in various situations. Have students provide key words, phrases, or gestures that act as "firecrackers" in stimulating a loss of self-control. For example, "When my boss rolls his eyes at me if I ask a question, I go ballistic" or "My boss tells me that I'm always late. I hate that!" Record their responses on the flip chart or white board.

◄ **Explain** that "firecrackers" tend to create a reaction in people that activates emotions. These emotions can be physically detected by a "pressure gauge" that measures increased stress and loss of control. Record on the flip chart or board the various "pressure gauge" reactions that students have noticed in themselves and others (i.e., sweaty palms, clenched fists, rapid breathing).

◄ **Hand out** the "I'm Going Off!" worksheet. Have students list different firecrackers that have set them off at home, at school, and at work (assuming they have worked in some capacity). After they have determined what firecrackers have set them off, have students begin thinking about the emotional or physical responses that register on their "pressure gauges."

◄ **Discuss** examples of firecrackers and pressure gauge reactions with the entire group.

WRAP-UP/HOMEWORK:

Ask students if they see a connection between the strategies presented in this lesson with operating from an internal locus of control. Tell them that maintaining self-control is critical to communicating effectively. Explain that later, during the communication unit, they will have an opportunity to practice their self-control in a "constructive communication" role-play.

Name _____

"I'm Going Off!"

Students should recall events and interactions that have occurred in three different settings: home, school, and workplace. They should list three "firecrackers" that have been ignited in each setting. The firecrackers should set off reactions that can be measured on their "pressure gauge." They should record the common reaction(s) to each firecracker in the pressure gauge section. For example, Firecracker = "My mom telling me to get off the phone, when she's been on it all evening." Pressure Gauge = "A knot in my stomach."

AT HOME

FIRECRACKERS: **PRESSURE GAUGE:**

1. _____   1. _____

2. _____   2. _____

3. _____   3. _____

AT SCHOOL

FIRECRACKERS: **PRESSURE GAUGE:**

4. _____   4. _____

5. _____   5. _____

6. _____   6. _____

AT WORK

FIRECRACKERS: **PRESSURE GAUGE:**

7. _____   7. _____

8. _____   8. _____

9. _____   9. _____

LESSON 7

Self-Control (Part Two)

PURPOSE	**THIS LESSON INTRODUCES STUDENTS TO ADDITIONAL STRATEGIES THAT WILL HELP THEM MAINTAIN SELF-CONTROL IN STRESSFUL SITUATIONS.** They will gain further knowledge about how these strategies help people operate from an internal locus of control. Students will not only recognize when they are beginning to "go off" but will practice methods of relaxation and affirmation through role-playing to maintain self-control.
LEARNING OUTCOMES	◀ Students will demonstrate a "cooling off" strategy in order to maintain self-control. ◀ Students will be able to identify at least two "affirmations" that contribute to sustaining self-control. ◀ Students will role-play an effective "cooling off" and "affirmation" scenario about avoiding a costly argument.
REVIEW (5 MINUTES)	Ask students what they do to maintain control when they are under stress. Explain how staying calm when others are frustrating, demeaning, or overbearing might save a relationship. Ask them for some examples of how they have coped with this kind of stress. As they talk about these events or situations attempt to help students understand the connection between locus of control and self-control. Continue to affirm that acting from an internal locus of control encourages people to demonstrate a higher level of self-control.
REQUIRED MATERIALS	◀ Flip chart or white board ◀ Argument Cue Cards ◀ "What Are Ya Gonna Do About It?" worksheet
LESSON 7 VOCABULARY	**HAVE STUDENTS REFER TO THEIR UNIT ONE/UNIT TWO VOCABULARY LIST AS YOU INTRODUCE THE FOLLOWING VOCABULARY WORDS AND PHRASES.** **Cooling Off:** What someone does to get things back under control. Example: counting to ten before responding to an insult. **Affirmation:** A personal statement or thought about oneself that is positive and hopeful. Example: having a thought like: "I am liked by my fellow employees," after your boss criticizes your work.

DESCRIPTION OF ACTIVITY:

ACTIVITY 7.1 **"WHAT ARE YA GONNA DO ABOUT IT?"** (25 MINUTES)

This activity will provide students with strategies to approach a "firecracker" with an internal locus of control. They will discuss and practice "cooling off" and "affirmations" as strategies to maintain self-control.

◄ **Ask** students to volunteer examples of techniques they use to "cool off" when they are thrown a firecracker. For example, "I leave the room for a few minutes" may be the way a student deals with a teacher. Record their responses on the flip chart or white board. Query students about what might be occurring to their locus of control in this "cool off" period (i.e., is it internal or external?).

◄ **Explain** that "affirmations" are meant to celebrate a person's strengths and capacities. Firecrackers tend to challenge the way we perceive ourselves, and affirmations help bring us back to a point of self-control. A good time to make affirmations is during the "cooling off" period. Ask for a few examples of affirmations that students have used (for example, "I have a great sense of humor" and "I am never late to work").

◄ **Hand out** the "What Are Ya Gonna Do About It?" Worksheet. Make sure that students understand that the "I'm Going Off!" Worksheet from the previous lesson will be necessary to complete the one being handed out. Ask them to record ways that they "cool off" and "affirmations" they might use to handle the firecrackers that were suggested on the "I'm Going Off!" Worksheet. Have students share their examples of "cooling off" and "affirmations."

ACTIVITY 7.2 **"FOR THE SAKE OF ARGUMENT"** (20 MINUTES)

This activity will provide students with an opportunity to model how "cooling off" and "affirmation" are effective strategies to avert exploding over firecrackers. Presented with various scenarios, students will role-play reactions to firecrackers that utilize these strategies and maintain an internal locus of control.

◄ **Divide** students into pairs and explain that they will be drawing from a deck of cards that sets the stage for disagreement, intimidation, and stress.

◄ Have each pair of students **draw a scenario** from the deck of Argument Cue Cards. Explain that they need to identify the firecracker presented by each card, and clarify how they will use a "cooling off" strategy and an "affirmation" to maintain self-control.

◄ Ask the pair to **role-play** these strategies as an effective means of demonstrating self-control and maintaining an internal locus of control.

WRAP-UP/HOMEWORK

Ask students if they see a connection between the strategies presented in this lesson and operating from an internal locus of control. Tell them that maintaining self-control is critical to communicating effectively. Explain that later, during the communication unit, they will have an opportunity to practice their self-control in a "constructive communication" role-play.

Name _____

"What Are Ya Gonna Do About It?"

Encourage students to use the "firecrackers" and "pressure gauge" responses from the previous lesson to determine one example of "cooling off" for each setting (home, school, work). Have them record two affirmations that would be useful across settings as they are cooling off.

1. **How can I "cool off" at:**
(*For example, "playing basketball" might be a good way to cool off at home.*)

Home?

School?

Work?

2. **List two "affirmations" that you can use across all settings.**
(*For example, "I have lots of friends."*)

Affirmation One:

Affirmation Two:

Argument Cue Cards

1.

Your math teacher has asked you to stay after school to talk about your failing grade. When you arrive at her office, she says, *"You need to realize what a disappointment you've been in this class."*

You want to respond with, *"You do a crappy job of explaining things!"*

2.

Your science teacher tells you, *"If you spent less time at work, and more time doing homework, you might graduate."*

You would like to respond with, *"Your class is a lot more boring than my job!"*

3.

Your employer has just denied you the opportunity to go home early so that you can study for a final exam. He says, *"You high school kids need to learn what responsibility is all about."*

You want to respond with, *"I'll bet you never finished high school!"*

4.

A coworker approaches you after you have reported him for harassment and says, *"You didn't have to report me. If you can't take what's dished out, find another job!"*

You would prefer to respond with, *"Maybe you need to understand what a jerk you are!"*

5.

A coworker has arrived late to work for the third time this week. Every time this happens, your crew gets penalized by not qualifying for a production bonus.

You want to tell him, *"Why don't you start thinking about somebody other than yourself?"*

6.

Your supervisor is never around when you have a question during your first days on the job. You ask a coworker how to work the "banding" machine for cardboard. When your supervisor sees you, he says, *"You have no business operating that dangerous piece of machinery!"*

You want to approach the coworker and ask her, *"Why didn't you tell me that I shouldn't be operating that piece of equipment?"*

7.

You are working with a roofing crew, and your supervisor has given you the toughest job: shoveling gravel onto the conveyor belt. This is normally a two-person job. By the afternoon break, you are exhausted.

At break, you want to tell him, *"You are not being fair to me!"*

8.

A coworker who is older than you keeps following you around, and it makes you feel uncomfortable. It seems like he is never working when you are.

You want to say, *"Aren't you supposed to be working somewhere?*

LESSON 8

Making More *W.A.G.E.S.*

PURPOSE	**DURING THIS LESSON STUDENTS WILL AGAIN PLAY THE "MAKING *W.A.G.E.S.*" GAME.**
	The game provides an opportunity to utilize the vocabulary and concepts covered over the remainder of the course. Students will become more familiar with the terminology associated with the foundation skills and attitudes of a successful employee and coworker.
LEARNING OUTCOMES	◄ Students will demonstrate increasing knowledge of the four foundation skills (i.e., Locus of Control, Teamwork, Communication, and Problem Solving) necessary to make successful connections on the job.
	◄ Students will demonstrate increasing knowledge of the attitudes (i.e., dependability, honesty, and enthusiasm) associated with effective social skills on the job.
REVIEW (5 MINUTES)	Ask students to recall the "Making *W.A.G.E.S.*" game that they played during Lesson 2. Show them the overheads on Foundation Skills and Attitudes from Lesson 2. Review the definitions of these vocabulary words, asking for student participation in recalling the meaning of each skill and quality.
REQUIRED MATERIALS	◄ Overheads (2) on Foundation Skills and Attitudes (from Lesson 2)
	◄ "Making *W.A.G.E.S.*" Game Cards (from Lesson 2)
	◄ "Making *W.A.G.E.S.*" Tally Sheet (from Lesson 2)
	◄ Treats or other incentives
	◄ Unit 2 Mastery Vocabulary Test (see Appendix)
LESSON 8 VOCABULARY	The vocabulary for this lesson is the same as Lesson 2 and can be found on the Foundation Skills and Attitudes overheads and on the Unit One/Unit Two Vocabulary List.

DESCRIPTION OF ACTIVITY:

ACTIVITY 8.1 **REVISITING THE "MAKING *W.A.G.E.S.*" GAME** (40 MINUTES)

This activity will allow students to compete for incentives by demonstrating their level of knowledge of course content. Students should be able to demonstrate a higher level of learning and performance than they did the first time they played.

- ◂ **Divide** students into teams (a maximum of three teams). Provide each team with a "Making *W.A.G.E.S.*" Tally Sheet that reflects the four content areas to be addressed in the course. A tally sheet reproducible is included at the end of Lesson 2.

- ◂ **Explain** to students that they will be asked to define or perform certain tasks (worth 100 to 500 points) contained on the back of cards in each of the four content areas. Tell them that the higher the number of points, the more difficult the problem. Also explain that the more difficult problems they answer, the more likely they are to earn more points than the other team. As teams choose cards and correctly answer the problems presented on the back of each card, members will keep track of points scored with each round played. It is a good idea for you to keep track of the points on the board or overhead, as well. In addition, you will need to judge students' performance on some of the questions to determine if they earned the points.

- ◂ **Requirements:** Each team will get one chance to solve each problem and earn points. Each team will be expected to select problems with varying point values for at least three rounds. They must choose problems with values that cannot be repeated until they have played three rounds (e.g., 100, 300, 200, then 100 is okay; 100, 200, 100 is not okay).

- ◂ The **Object** of the game is to score the highest number of points in the amount of time available. Hint: A student choosing to answer easier questions for fewer points will stand a better chance of earning points (especially during the first time the game is played), but higher points are scored for answering fewer hard questions/problems. At the end of play, total points earned throughout the game determine the winner. Incentives for the winners should be given (e.g., free time, treats, etc.).

MASTERY TEST (5 MINUTES)

Give students the Unit 2 Mastery Vocabulary Test and time them for five minutes. Chart student progress later using whatever system your school prefers.

WRAP-UP/HOMEWORK

Inform students that they will get to play the "Making *W.A.G.E.S.*" game one more time during Unit Four: Problem Solving. They should be much more capable of performing tasks and answering questions of a higher value at that point. Ask for student feedback on the game. Is it a fun way to learn? What types of incentives would they like for the next time they play?

UNIT

3

LESSONS 9–13

TEAMWORK

UNIT 3

LESSON 9

Teamwork

PURPOSE	**THIS LESSON INTRODUCES (A) THE CONCEPT OF TEAMWORK AND (B) THE QUALITIES AND CHARACTERISTICS THAT ARE NECESSARY TO ENGAGE IN PRODUCTIVE TEAMWORK.** Through a brainstorming session and a fun, hands-on activity, students will learn about the importance of teamwork on the job.
LEARNING OUTCOMES:	◄ After participating in activities that articulate qualities of teamwork, students will be able to identify at least four qualities of effective teamwork that were or were not modeled in the activities. ◄ After participating in activities that articulate the roles of team members, students will be able to identify roles assumed by members of the team.
REVIEW	There is no review for this lesson.
REQUIRED MATERIALS	◄ Flip chart ◄ A one-gallon coffee can (This can should be perforated in random locations—seven holes is ideal—and laced with varying lengths of twine secured by knotted ends. No piece of twine should be the same length—some should be longer and some should be shorter. The knots should secure the twine on the inside of the can, with the length of the twine extending outward from the holes in the can.) ◄ One five-pound bag of pinto beans ◄ One foil turkey pan ◄ One small plastic bowl (6–8 oz.) ◄ Stopwatch or other timer ◄ Qualities of Teamwork worksheet
LESSON 9 VOCABULARY	There is no new vocabulary for this lesson. Do, however, hand out the Unit Three Vocabulary List (see Appendix).

DESCRIPTION OF ACTIVITY

ACTIVITY 9.1   **"WHAT IS TEAMWORK, ANYWAY?"** (10 MINUTES)

In this activity students will brainstorm the many qualities of teamwork and compile them into a class list.

◄ **Pair students up** and instruct them to, as a team, generate as many qualities of teamwork as they can in five minutes. Tell them they should be able to come up with at least 10 qualities. As a time-saving alternative, the entire class can generate qualities together as you record them on the flip chart.

◄ **Provide examples** as necessary (for example, "leadership," "cooperation," "patience," "communication," "sense of humor," "working together," "trust," "compromise," etc.).

◄ **Report to the large group** the attitudes, qualities, and behaviors associated with teamwork, if you did not generate the list as a large group already.

◄ **Record** all of the information on a flip chart or board. Keep this information for Lesson 10.

◄ **Inform** students that the next activity will allow them to experience many of the qualities of teamwork and that their list will be revisited after the activity concludes.

ACTIVITY 9.2   **"DON'T SPILL THE BEANS!"** (30 MINUTES)

This activity will allow students to experience hands-on the qualities of teamwork they just generated. Students usually give much positive feedback about this activity.

◄ **Make sure** there is a lot of room for his activity. Moving the desks out of the way or going outside may be necessary.

◄ **Divide** students into teams of seven, or however many strands are attached to the one-gallon coffee can.

◄ **Ask** students to choose a name for their teams, and write the names of the teams on the board.

◄ **Explain** to students that they will be asked to perform three teamwork tasks with the bean can and that their performance will be assessed by time and by the amount of beans spilled completing the tasks. Have each team circle the bean can and go over the following rules:

1. Each member must grasp the end of a strand of twine (they cannot hold the strand anywhere other than at its very end).

2. At no point during the completion of their tasks can they utilize their other hand to shorten their strands and guide the can.

3. Time starts when the can moves, and stops when the can is sitting in the desired location.

◄ **Have each team** coordinate the lifting of the can so that it is held level at all times. After each team has practiced raising the can, flip a coin to see (or decide in some other fashion) which team will go first. From this point have the teams take turns performing the following tasks:

    a. With the can half full of pinto beans, have the team move the can to the top of a table at a prearranged location.

    b. With the can completely filled, have each team move the can to the tabletop.

    c. With the can completely filled, have each team move the can to the table and pour the beans into a plastic bowl until the bowl is half full (this bowl should be in the middle of the foil turkey pan so that you can easily count the beans that fall into the pan).

◄ **Keep track** of the elapsed time, using a stopwatch or other timing device, and the amount of beans spilled during the completion of each task. Reward each team for effort, and determine a winner for each task by comparing the speeds of the teams with the number of beans they dropped during the task.

◄ **Explain** that the next activity will allow the students to think about the characteristics of teamwork they just observed or used while completing the bean-carry task.

ACTIVITY 9.3   **QUALITIES OF TEAMWORK WORKSHEET** (5–10 MINUTES)

This activity will allow students to demonstrate in writing their knowledge of the qualities of teamwork.

◄ **Have** students complete the Qualities of Teamwork worksheet by correctly identifying at least four qualities of teamwork that were evident in the work of their teams. They must provide examples of where and when these qualities were noticed.

WRAP-UP/HOMEWORK

Inform students that homework will be to bring back three examples of teamwork that they have experienced or observed in the community. They can write these examples on notebook paper.

Name_____

Qualities of Teamwork

Identify the teamwork qualities you observed during the bean-can activity, and explain where in the activity you saw that quality (the evidence).

TEAMWORK QUALITY	EVIDENCE

Which of the above qualities was the most important to your team?

List any qualities that you wish your team had had during the activity.

LESSON **10**

Good Values Are Out of This World!

PURPOSE	**THIS LESSON POINTS OUT HOW INDIVIDUAL VALUES TEND TO INFLUENCE DECISIONS MADE BY A TEAM.** In this simulation activity, students will become members of a four-person team faced with making decisions based on their individual values. They will practice self-advocacy skills and consensus reaching as they argue and lobby for those persons they feel are most qualified to depart from this dying planet and begin a new world on Mars.
LEARNING OUTCOMES	◀ Students will demonstrate the ability to accept the opinions and values of others in order to reach agreement. ◀ Students will demonstrate the ability to effectively advocate for their own set of values as a member of a team.
REVIEW (5 MINUTES)	Hand out the list of teamwork qualities that were generated in Lesson 9 and explain that the activity that the students are about to engage in will allow them to practice some of the qualities they perceived as important to a team. As you go through the list of qualities, attempt to highlight those qualities that illuminate assertiveness and consensus as effective team dynamics. Explain that the activity in which they are about to participate will rely on these qualities.
REQUIRED MATERIALS	◀ Teamwork Qualities List (this is the class list of teamwork qualities generated in Lesson 9) ◀ A New World Journey vignette handout ◀ Satisfaction Survey
LESSON 10 VOCABULARY	**HAVE STUDENTS REFER TO THEIR UNIT TWO VOCABULARY LIST AS YOU INTRODUCE THE FOLLOWING VOCABULARY WORDS.** **Self-Advocacy:** A person's ability to speak up, defend, or promote his or her opinion or belief. Example: being able to let a coworker know they are letting down the team by being late to work. **Consensus:** When every member of a group is willing to go along with the general feeling of the group. For example, Ted may not particularly agree with his two friends, but they were so excited that he went along with their desires.

DESCRIPTION OF ACTIVITY

ACTIVITY 10.1 A NEW WORLD JOURNEY (45 MINUTES)

This fun activity will allow students to experience decision making and values clarification as a team. They will determine what types of people would best be sent to Mars to start a new colony of the human race.

◄ **Form teams** of four students who have varied interests and perspectives. This will allow the activity to proceed according to the differences in values each member brings to the discussion. Assign one person to be the secretary, one person to be the group discussion leader, and two people to be spokepersons for the group.

◄ **Hand out** the New World Journey vignette and together read the narrative that defines the ground rules for departing on the "new world journey."

◄ **Explain that they will have 15–20 minutes** to decide, from a list of 14 potential astronauts, which six will be allowed to start a new life on Mars. They must provide positive supporting evidence for their choices. Negative put-downs should not be tolerated.

◄ **At the conclusion** of the 15–20 minutes, two team members will be charged with reporting back to the large group on the astronauts who have been selected for the journey and the reasons behind the choices. Again, they need to provide positive supporting evidence.

◄ **If possible**, attempt to reach consensus with the larger group on which six astronauts should make the flight.

WRAP-UP/HOMEWORK: (5 MINUTES)

As homework, or preferably in class if time allows, poll students with the Satisfaction Survey to determine their level of satisfaction with the group's process. Did they find themselves locked out of the decision making by the committee? What would they rate the level of consensus to be among committee members? Generate a quick discussion if time allows.

A New World Journey

The Year is 2017, and you have been appointed to a team for the purpose of developing a passenger list to create new life on the planet Mars. The earth has finally worn out, due to global warming and the depletion of the ozone layer in the atmosphere. Scientists are predicting that, by the end of the year, life will begin to disintegrate at an alarming rate and that, by the year 2020, mankind will no longer exist. The world is gearing up for this tremendous shutdown with much confusion and anxiety.

NASA has made a decision to deliver a crew of six Earthlings to the planet Mars, because past research on its atmosphere and geography offers hope for the future. A total of 14 candidates representing a cross-section of humanity have been trained for the journey. Only six will be allowed to depart in the fully automated starship. The purpose of the mission is to create and sustain life on the new planet as life is extinguished on earth. Your committee must decide which of the 14 astronauts will qualify for the team of six. The decision of your committee must represent the consensus of the group. Every member is expected to contribute an important part to the decision-making. Two of your members will be expected to report back to the Worldwide Civil Liberties Union on those astronauts who are chosen for the trek to Mars. Here is the list of potential passengers:

1. A French woman who is 29 years old and can speak seven languages. She has always wanted to be a teacher. She has been divorced twice and has never had children.

2. A 25-year-old female heptathlete. After immigrating to the United States from Mexico two years ago, she qualified to compete in the world championships for her native country. She was unfairly disqualified for taking steroids.

3. A 15-year-old white high school student from Oregon. She is from a poor family in a small rural town. Since moving into the city to live with her uncle, she has done well socially and is working part-time at a local fast food franchise.

A New World Journey (continued)

4. A 55-year-old clergyman from Germany. He is renowned for his sense of humor and his ability to make good wine. He recently lost his wife in an automobile accident.

5. A 36-year-old female physician from Australia. She is currently engaged for the first time in her life. She is unable to have children.

6. A 26-year-old Stanford law student who is from the Philippines. He enjoys basketball and hockey. He and his wife are expecting their first child in the fall.

7. The law student's 29-year-old wife who spent the last two months in a rehabilitation center suffering from severe depression. She relies heavily on her husband for support and encouragement.

8. A 14-year-old female exchange student from Africa. She can speak only limited English. Her family is well established because her father is the CEO of a large multinational corporation that produces computer software in her home country of Kenya.

9. A 48-year-old computer specialist from New Jersey who is Native American. His specialty is designing programs that support the technology needs of developing rural communities. He is the first in his family to graduate from college.

10. A 32-year-old female architect from Italy. She is a single parent. Her work with environmental shelters has made her world-renowned. She specializes in developing caves into livable dwellings.

11. A 40-year-old male marine biologist from the United Kingdom. His work with fungi led to his being awarded a Nobel Prize in science. He has a reputation for being an elitist.

12. A 24-year-old American rodeo star. He has been raised on a ranch for most of his life and has no desire to start a family. He is a terrific mechanic.

13. An entrepreneur from Russia who has made it big in the American stock market. He is 51 years old and unmarried. He is confined to a wheelchair.

14. A 37-year-old astronaut who was born in Japan and immigrated to the U.S. with his family. He is a vegetarian. He has never been married. He has control issues with other crew members.

Satisfaction Survey

You _____

Other Team Members: _____

_____

_____

Circle Your Responses

1. To what extent do you feel your group members listened to your point of view?

    1—Not at all   **2—A little**   **3—Quite a bit**   **4—Completely**

2. How difficult was it to reach consensus in your group?

    1—Very difficult   **2—Somewhat difficult**   **3—Not too difficult**   **4—Very easy**

3. How satisfied were you with your group's final decision?

    1—Not at all   **2—A little**   **3—Mostly**   **4—Completely**

4. To what extent do you feel your group's final decision was a consensus of the group members' opinions?

    1—Not at all   **2—A little**   **3—Mostly**   **4—Completely**

5. Overall, how satisfied were you with how your group members worked together?

    1—Not at all   **2—A little**   **3—Mostly**   **4—Completely**

6. What was your role on the team?

    Secretary   **Discussion Leader**   **Spokesperson**

7. Do you have any additional comments about your group?

LESSON 11

"What's in the Bag?"

PURPOSE	**THIS LESSON PROVIDES A FUN OPPORTUNITY FOR STUDENTS—IN SEPARATE TEAMS—TO PLAN, REHEARSE, AND PRESENT A SKIT.** Given a paper bag full of random props, each team will use creativity and shared responsibility to present an entertaining skit.
LEARNING OUTCOMES	◀ Students will demonstrate creativity and cooperation as a member of a team. ◀ Students will demonstrate shared responsibility and a defined role as a member of a team.
REVIEW (5 MINUTES)	Discuss with students the importance of building consensus and unity within a team. Reflect on the decision-making that occurred in determining the six passengers who would make the journey to develop a new world on Mars (Lesson 10). Probe students about their level of satisfaction in being represented by the final decision. Explain that the team decision-making that occurred in the New World Journey vignette was primarily to analyze a problem and reach consensus. Today's activity will allow them to be more creative in their roles and decision-making as they cooperatively design a short skit.
REQUIRED MATERIALS	◀ Paper bags ◀ Five props per bag (containing items from home, school, work that are convenient to collect—see the suggested list of props for ideas) ◀ A Suggested List of Props & Themes for Brown Bag Skits sheet
LESSON 11 VOCABULARY	**HAVE STUDENTS REFER TO THEIR UNIT TWO VOCABULARY LIST AS YOU INTRODUCE THE FOLLOWING VOCABULARY WORDS.** **Prop:** An article used in a skit/play to make the setting or action seem more realistic. Examples: an eye patch worn to define the role of a pirate, or a tie-dyed shirt to define the role of a 60's hippie.

Description of Activity

Activity 11.1   What's In The Bag? (40 MINUTES)

This activity provides an entertaining context in which students can further their learning about teamwork.

- ◄ **Divide** students into teams of five.
- ◄ **Distribute** a paper bag with props to each team.
- ◄ **Review** the following expectations with the group:
    - Each team will be given a theme to use as they create a 2–3 minute skit for the group. You can help explain the theme to each group if they do not understand the meaning or intent of the theme.
    - Teams must use *all* of the props in the bag.
    - Each team member must have a role in the play.
    - Teams will have 15 minutes to design, rehearse, and refine their skit.
- ◄ **You might** want to provide some teams with space outside the classroom to rehearse their skits. If teams are outside of the classroom, it will be important to monitor them in a consistent manner.
- ◄ **Introduce** each skit by theme and provide positive support to teams as they present.

Wrap-Up/Homework (5 MINUTES)

After all teams have performed their skits, discuss the value of each team member having a role in the production. More than likely, teams will have been creative and humorous in the design of their presentations. This is a good time to emphasize the importance of humor and fun in building a strong team. Ask students if they can think of examples of teams that have profited from humor and fun.

A Suggested List of
Props & Themes for Brown Bag Skits

tie	glasses	watch	detergent
bow tie	belt	suspenders	badge
golf hat	handcuffs	rope	calculator
baseball cap	spoon	harmonica	novel/book
pen	phone	beeper	ball
pop bottle	keyboard	alarm clock	marker
food container	dictionary	whistle	flashlight
clothes hanger	banana	headband	bat
leash	lab coat	hard hat	walkman
videotape	notebook	ruler	date book
candle	mouse pad	extension cord	screwdriver
key	stapler	paper clip	transparent tape

Themes For Brown Bag Skits

"Enthusiasm is difficult to find in the workplace."

"Honesty is critical in the workplace."

"Accepting criticism is not an easy thing to do."

"Asking questions is very important to doing a job right."

"Self-control is not an easy thing to have."

"Problem solving is an important job skill."

"Self-advocacy is important on the job."

"The customer is always right."

"Harassment in the workplace doesn't cut it."

"Teams that play together stay together."

LESSON 12

What's in a Team?

PURPOSE	**THIS LESSON PROVIDES ADDITIONAL OPPORTUNITIES FOR STUDENTS TO GAIN A BROADER PERSPECTIVE OF TEAMWORK.** By participating in two more activities that demand group decision-making and cooperation, students will apply the principles of effective teamwork in a highly recreational lesson.
LEARNING OUTCOMES	◀ After participating in two activities that articulate qualities of teamwork, students will be able to identify at least five qualities of effective teamwork.
REVIEW (5 MINUTES)	Hand out the list of teamwork qualities that was generated in Lesson 9 and explain that the activities in which they are about to participate will emphasize many of the items on the list. Have students vote on the top five (most important on the job) qualities on the list. Rank and order the top five before moving on to the activities in this lesson.
REQUIRED MATERIALS	◀ Teamwork Qualities List (prepared from items generated in Lesson 9) ◀ Flip chart or white board ◀ Qualities of Teamwork worksheet ◀ CBM Vocabulary Test #3
LESSON 12 VOCABULARY	There is no new vocabulary for this lesson.

DESCRIPTION OF ACTIVITY

ACTIVITY 12.1   THE HUMAN KNOT (15–45 MINUTES)

This engaging and enjoyable activity will test students' abilities to problem solve a difficult situation using teamwork.

- ◄ **Form** teams of eight students.

- ◄ **Tell** students to form circles near the center of the room. Explain to them that the following activity will involve a high degree of movement and potential physical contact, which requires respect, sensitivity, and discretion.

- ◄ **Tighten** the circles enough for everyone to reach across to a partner on the other side with their right hand.

- ◄ **Tell** students they cannot break the grip with the person whom they are connected.

- ◄ **Have** them connect their left hand with another person in the group, so that they are grasping two different partners, neither of whom is directly next to them.

- ◄ **The Object** of this activity is to untie the knot they have created by moving around, through, and over one another to form a continuous circle. They need to do this without ever breaking their grip with either partner.

- ◄ **If they untie** themselves too quickly, have them redo the activity. Make sure they are quite tangled before they begin untying themselves again.

- ◄ **This activity** may take from a few minutes to the entire class session. At some point, have students return to their seats and complete the Qualities of Teamwork worksheet. Using the Teamwork Qualities List, have them record the qualities they experienced or observed in the Human Knot activity. They should decide as a group if they believe the five top qualities they generated earlier should be revised or reordered.

ACTIVITY 12.2   CIRCLE SIT (15–20 MINUTES)

Allowing the students to do the Human Knot activity for the entire period can be highly rewarding if the students are productively engaged. However, we have provided another team activity if time allows.

- ◄ **Students** should remain on the same team for this activity. Caution students that the following activity demands the same level of respect and discretion as the Human Knot.

- ◄ **Have them** form circles of eight or more near the middle of the room.

- ◄ **Every person** in the circle should be facing the same direction. They should eventually form a continuous circle, tight enough to be within an arm's length of the person in front of them.

◀ **The Object** of this activity is to have all team members sit on the knees of the person who is positioned directly behind them. They should create a continuous circle supporting one another in a chair-sit position for at least 15 seconds.

Caution: Explain that everyone is at risk of injuring a tailbone or bruising their derriere if they are reckless about accomplishing the group task.

◀ Teams may need to try this activity more than one time. It is possible to modify the activity by having teams compete to sustain the circle for the longest period of time. At the conclusion of the Circle Sit activity, discuss the teamwork qualities that were experienced or observed in the completion of the task.

CBM (10 MINUTES)

Hand out the CBM Vocabulary Test #3 to the students. Time them for seven minutes, then collect their tests. Use the results as a guide to student progress on vocabulary concepts.

WRAP-UP/HOMEWORK

Revisit the Teamwork Qualities List if necessary, and revise any qualities that may be added to or deleted from the top five choices of the group. Tell students to bring back a written example of teamwork occurring in the workplace, based on at least one of the top five qualities. Explain that teamwork may not be quite as much fun in the workplace as in these activities but that the same qualities are still there.

Name _____

Qualities of Teamwork

Identify the teamwork qualities you observed during the activity, and explain where in the activity you saw that quality (the evidence).

TEAMWORK QUALITY	EVIDENCE

Which of the above qualities was the most important to your team?

List any qualities that you wish your team had had during the activity.

UNIT
3

LESSON 13

Practice Makes Perfect

PURPOSE	THIS LESSON PROVIDES TWO MORE RECREATIONAL OPPORTUNITIES FOR STUDENTS TO EXPERIENCE PROBLEM SOLVING AS A MEMBER OF A TEAM.
	The two activities introduced in this lesson emphasize the importance of cooperation and communication in building successful teams.
LEARNING OUTCOMES	◀ After participating in two activities that articulate qualities of teamwork, students will be able to describe how cooperation and communication are necessary for team success.
REVIEW (5 MINUTES)	Have students report examples of teamwork in the workplace that they have observed or experienced since completing Lesson 9 or that they can recall from the recent past. Relate their observations to the top five teamwork qualities identified in the last lesson.
REQUIRED MATERIALS	◀ Qualities of Teamwork worksheet (completed with top five choices from Lesson 12)
	◀ Several pieces of material (paper, plastic, cloth) with dimensions that approximate a 10' x 12' rectangle
	◀ 15 feet of yarn
	◀ Two chairs
	◀ A stopwatch or something to keep time with
	◀ Unit 3 Mastery Vocabulary Test
LESSON 13 VOCABULARY	There is no new vocabulary for this lesson.

DESCRIPTION OF ACTIVITY

ACTIVITY 13.1   COLLAPSING ELEVATOR (15 MINUTES)

This activity provides yet another fun and engaging context in which students can practice and recognize what they have learned about teamwork.

- ◄ Form teams of 5–8 students (teams should have an equal number of students).
- ◄ Distribute 10' x 12' material to each team.
- ◄ Explain:
    - All team members must be standing on the material.
    - They must remain on the material without making contact with the floor outside of the material for at least 15 seconds.
- ◄ **Begin** by having teams stand on the entire sheet of material.
- ◄ **Progressively** begin folding material in half decreasing available space with each round.
- ◄ **The Object** of this activity is to keep the maximum number of team members on the smallest amount of material for at least 15 seconds.
- ◄ **Reward** the team(s) that keeps their team members on the smallest amount of material for at least 15 seconds.
- ◄ **Discuss** the value of relying on one another to strengthen the performance of the team. What other qualities of teamwork contributed to success?

ACTIVITY 13.2   LIVE WIRE (15–20 MINUTES)

If time allows, the same teams can play this entertaining game.

- ◄ **Form teams** of five or more students.
- ◄ **Extend** the 15-foot ball of yarn between the two chairs; tie off so that the yarn is taut between the backs of both chairs. This is the "live wire."
- ◄ The **Object** is for each team to get every team member over the live wire without contacting the yarn in a designated period of time. Speed is important.

Expectations:

- Everyone starts out on one side of the yarn.
- Students must pass over the yarn without touching.
- If a member contacts the yarn, the entire team must start over.
- Teams cannot stand on backs of teammates or throw others over the wire.

◀ The **winning team** is the team that takes the least amount of time to get every team member over the live wire without touching it.

◀ **Discuss** the strategies employed by the various teams in accomplishing their mission. What qualities of teamwork were evident?

MASTERY TEST (5 MINUTES)

Give students the Unit 3 Mastery Vocabulary Test and time them for five minutes. Record scores later.

WRAP-UP/HOMEWORK

Ask students about experiences that may have occurred in their lives where they have had to work as a team, supporting other members in the accomplishment of a task or duty. Cite pertinent examples of teamwork that have been evident in school, community, and workplace settings (e.g., a fund-raising car wash, trauma support to a local high school, or coordinated efforts between restaurant staff). Inquire about the manner and degree of communication that was necessary to accomplish such tasks. Inform students that the next unit will further develop common elements of effective communication.

(Credit for the two activities described in this lesson goes to Naomi Rombaoa, who was a University of Oregon student intern.)

UNIT
4

LESSONS 14–24

COMMUNICATION

Lesson 14

Did I Hear You Right?

PURPOSE	**THIS LESSON INTRODUCES THE CONCEPT OF COMMUNICATION IN THE WORKPLACE.** Through a hands-on activity and a homework assignment, this lesson emphasizes the importance of effective communication and its relationship to effective teamwork and an internal locus of control.
COMPLEMENTARY ACTIVITIES	At some point during Unit Four, schedule time for the résumé building, letter writing, and other activities suggested in Table 3 of the Instructor's Guide.
LEARNING OUTCOMES	◄ After participating in a one-way vs. two-way communication activity, students will be able to explain the advantages of two-way communication. ◄ Students will be able to relate the importance of communication to the workplace.
REQUIRED MATERIALS	◄ Paper cups filled with small objects. Each cup should have contents identical to the other cups. (Examples include ice cream bar sticks, marbles, colored rings, etc. Different-colored objects make it more challenging.) ◄ Manila folders (to act as a partition between two players) ◄ Unit Four Vocabulary List
LESSON 14 VOCABULARY	**HAVE STUDENTS REFER TO THE UNIT FOUR VOCABULARY LIST AS YOU INTRODUCE THE FOLLOWING VOCABULARY TERMS.** **One-Way Communication:** When one person is doing all of the talking and no one else asks questions or interacts with the person. **Two-Way Communication:** When people interact, listen, and ask questions of one another to clearly understand what is said. **Nonverbal Communication:** What an individual says with his or her body, facial expressions, tone of voice, and posture. Slumped shoulders, no eye contact, crossed arms, a low voice, and fidgeting are examples of nonverbal communication that should be avoided during an interview. Eye contact, smiling, a clear voice, and good posture are examples of nonverbal communication that should be utilized during an interview.

DESCRIPTION OF ACTIVITY

ACTIVITY 14.1   ARE YOU HEARING ME? (45 MINUTES)

This activity will allow students to experience the importance of two-way communication in the workplace, as opposed to one-way communication. In addition, they will begin to recognize the importance of nonverbal communication.

◄ **Inform students** that they are moving into a new unit on Communication, which will build upon what they have learned in the previous units on Locus of Control and Teamwork.

◄ **Tell students** that they need to team into pairs, sitting across the table from one another. Each student will be given a cup full of identical items. One of the students will be expected to design a structure or an arrangement of items using all of the materials, including the cup. The other student will be expected to construct an exact replica of their partner's model, including color, by simply *listening* to the directions.

◄ **Emphasize** to students the importance of *not* asking questions or trying to get additional information when they are being given directions. Upon completion of the task, have students compare their arrangements. Wait until all partners are done, then have them switch roles and repeat the exercise (although the other partner cannot build the same structure).

◄ The **next task** for the pairs will be to construct a new structure or arrangement (not the same as the first or second one) and provide directions to their partners. This time the person being given directions can ask questions and attempt to get additional information, without looking at the structure. This task need only be done once per pair of students, unless time allows for an exchange of roles.

◄ Discuss the difference between the first and second tasks based on one-way vs. two-way communication. Also, discuss how nonverbal communication came into play (e.g., puzzled looks, shaking head, etc.). What meaning does this have for the workplace?

– How might this situation arise in the workplace?

– What might two-way communication have to do with following directions?

– What is difficult about asking questions when dealing with a boss?

WRAP-UP/HOMEWORK

Attempt to impress students with the importance of two-way communication in light of what they have already learned about teamwork and responsibility (LOC). Explain how lack of effective communication oftentimes impacts teams and causes people to act externally ("moaning"). Assign students the task of bringing in *three* examples where people have acted internally or externally due to effective or ineffective communication.

LESSON 15

Communication Breakdown

PURPOSE	**THIS LESSON ELABORATES ON THE ISSUES OF ONE-WAY VS. TWO-WAY COMMUNICATION AND NONVERBAL COMMUNICATION THAT WERE INTRODUCED IN LESSON 14.**
	Through an activity that has been given positive reviews from many students, your students will experience the frustration and confusion that often follows unclear communication.
LEARNING OUTCOMES	◄ As a group, students will be able to identify at least 15 qualities of communication that employers look for in their employees.
	◄ After participating in the "telephone game" activity, students will be able to identify at least three reasons why communication sometimes breaks down.
REVIEW	Briefly review with students the significance of one-way, two-way, and nonverbal communication, and go over some of the LOC homework examples the students were asked to bring in. Ask them to recall the cup game played in Lesson 14 and how the different forms of communication came into play. Explain that today's lesson will focus on the importance of making communication clear and ensuring that it makes sense to the other people we work with.
REQUIRED MATERIALS	◄ A flip chart or white board/chalkboard
	◄ Communication Breakdown Worksheet
LESSON 15 VOCABULARY	There is no new vocabulary for this lesson.

DESCRIPTION OF ACTIVITY

ACTIVITY 15.1 QUALITIES OF COMMUNICATION (10 MINUTES)

This activity will allow students to focus on a variety of important aspects, or qualities, of communication.

◄ As a group, ask students to identify as many qualities of communication that employers look for in their employees as they can. Record these responses on a flip chart or board.

◄ Give examples as needed: "smiling," "good posture," "firm handshake," "being nice to others," "not interrupting," "dressing appropriately," "positive attitude," "asking questions," etc.

◄ Emphasize to the students that virtually everything they do communicates something to the people around them.

ACTIVITY 15.2 TELEPHONE GAME (30–40 MINUTES)

This activity will allow students to experience involvement in a communication network that uses unclear vs. clear communication.

◄ Tell students they will be participating in an activity much like the game called "telephone" or "operator" they might have played as children.

◄ Explain the following rules.

– Teams can be as small as 6–8 people or as large as the entire class. The larger the group, the more challenging the exercise.

– The students should be set up in a circle or horseshoe shape.

– You will start the game by whispering a sentence to the first person. The more confusing the sentence, the better, although you should adjust the confusion level to the abilities of your students and limit the number of words to six or seven. Here are some examples of sentences:

• "Proper articulation makes for coordinated effort."

• "Crying babies glow with sunshine and diapers."

• "Educational supervision cries for mammoths and artists."

• "Floppy bunnies wish for chocolate manicures."

– Each student whispers what they heard to the next student, without others hearing.

– Each student may repeat the sentence to the next person only one time (two times total). Then the next person *must* tell it to the next person, and so forth.

- When the final student in the group has heard the sentence, he or she says it out loud to the class. Hopefully, the sentence will *not* be the original sentence.

◄ Quickly trace the sentence back through the students, asking each student what he thought he heard. This questioning will show where the communication breakdown occurred.

◄ Ask students why they think the communication breakdown occurred. Some possible reasons include:

- Not being able to ask questions.

- Only using one-way communication.

- Whispering rather than talking.

- The sentence did not make sense.

- The sentence did not pertain to the activity at hand.

◄ Repeat the game several times, using different confusing sentences. You can vary the game by starting the sentence at two different ends of the horseshoe or circle and seeing what the two middle students come up with as the sentence they heard. Always examine the communication breakdown.

◄ Finally, play the game one more time. This time, however, use a sentence that makes complete sense to the game and is fairly simple. Ideas include:

- "Don't forget to listen with your ears."

- "Whisper softly so no one will hear."

◄ Hopefully, the students will nail this one on the head, or at least come very close. Ask them why this happened. They should be able to identify:

- The sentence was clear.

- The sentence seemed shorter.

- The words were simpler and easier to understand.

- The sentence pertained to the game they were playing.

WRAP-UP/HOMEWORK

Emphasize the importance of keeping your sentences clear and easy to foster understanding when communicating in the workplace. Reinforce students for their participation in the telephone game. Ask them for feedback. Did they enjoy the game? Do they feel they learned about communication? Hand out the Communication Breakdown Worksheet and ask them to bring back at least three reasons why communication sometimes breaks down.

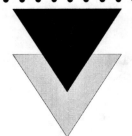

Name _____

Communication Breakdown Worksheet

During the telephone game activity, you experienced breakdowns in communication among group members. Think back to that activity. Identify at least three reasons why communication sometimes breaks down between people.

1. _____

_____

2. _____

_____

3. _____

_____

Develop your own personal motto (words to live by) regarding ways to maintain good communication in the workplace.

_____

_____

LESSON 16

Could You Repeat That?

PURPOSE	**THIS LESSON ALLOWS STUDENTS THE OPPORTUNITY TO LINK COMMUNICATION BREAKDOWNS TO PROBLEMS IN THE WORKPLACE.** The ability to follow directions is dependent upon the sender and the receiver of information being on the same wavelength. In this exercise, students will explore the effects of paraphrasing as a technique for encouraging a clear understanding between two people.
LEARNING OUTCOMES	◀ Students will be able to demonstrate the ability to use paraphrasing (i.e., restating another person's position) as an advocacy skill to clarify directions.
REVIEW (5 MINUTES)	Have students refer to the Communication Breakdown Worksheets that were assigned in Lesson 15 as they discuss the reasons communication breaks down between people. Ask for volunteers to tell examples of mottos that may help to maintain good communication in the workplace. Explain that today's lesson will deal with effective ways of communicating so that people can follow directions in the workplace.
REQUIRED MATERIALS	◀ Communication Breakdown Worksheet from Lesson 15 ◀ Crystal Clear Communication Worksheet ◀ "Clear as a Bell?" Paraphrasing Log
LESSON 16 VOCABULARY	**HAVE STUDENTS REFER TO THEIR UNIT FOUR VOCABULARY LIST AS YOU INTRODUCE THE FOLLOWING VOCABULARY WORD.** **Paraphrase:** A communication style where you state in your own words what you thought someone just said. Examples: "Do you mean the primer needs to dry for two hours before I begin finishing the trim?" or "Are you telling me that I should have waited to begin mopping the floor?"

DESCRIPTION OF ACTIVITY

ACTIVITY 16.1 **CRYSTAL CLEAR COMMUNICATION** (15–20 MINUTES)

This activity will introduce students to the concept of paraphrasing to clarify what someone says. Students will work in pairs to practice paraphrasing what their partners say.

◄ **Model** an example of paraphrasing by asking one or two students to volunteer talking about their favorite activity in this class to date. Ask them to tell why it is their favorite. Use paraphrasing to understand clearly *why* the student enjoyed the activity.

For example, "I liked the bean-can activity. We all learned how to work together as a team. It was fun even when we spilled the beans."

Paraphrase: "So, you enjoyed the bean-can activity because you liked working together as a team, even if it meant having to pick up spilled beans? What was so special about this sort of activity?"

◄ **Pair** students up.

◄ **Have each pair** practice paraphrasing each other by discussing an example of when a teacher or an employer made them angry. Use paraphrasing to understand why they got angry. For example: "Mrs. Smith counted me tardy one day when I was in my seat before class even started. She wouldn't believe that I was there on time. She really made me angry." Paraphrase: "Mrs. Smith made you angry because she counted you tardy when you were already in class?"

◄ **Ask for volunteers** to present their examples in a role-play fashion. Give additional examples of paraphrasing if the class seems to need more instruction.

◄ **Emphasize** the importance of paraphrasing to clarify what your boss or supervisor tells you to do. Explain that when you tell the boss what you think you heard him or her say, then your boss can tell you if you heard the directions correctly or not. This reduces the chances you will make a mistake when attempting to follow directions.

ACTIVITY 16.2 **CRYSTAL CLEAR COMMUNICATION** (20 MINUTES)

This activity will allow students, in pairs, to practice paraphrasing directions or statements a boss or coworker might give or say on the job.

◄ **Distribute** two Crystal Clear Communication Worksheets to each pair and ask them to paraphrase the four statements made by supervisors and coworkers. Each student should fill out a worksheet.

◄ **Discuss** each statement as a large group. Solicit examples of paraphrasing that the pairs devised for each statement.

◄ Have everyone turn in their worksheets.

WRAP-UP/HOMEWORK

Give students copies of the "Clear as a Bell?" Paraphrasing Log to use in recording an example of how they used effective paraphrasing at home, work, or school. Tell them that role-playing a couple of examples of paraphrasing will be how the next lesson begins.

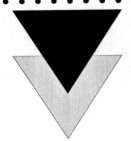

Name _____

Crystal Clear Communication Worksheet

Write down a statement or statements that would adequately paraphrase these common workplace comments:

1. **Supervisor to employee:** "Before you send an e-mail attachment make sure that you have saved the attachment in a rich text format and alerted the receiving party in the body of your message that there is an attachment."

   Paraphrase: "I should _____

   _____

   _____

2. **Coworker to coworker:** "You can forward voice mail messages by first hitting the recall button on your touch-tone phone, then dialing the extension you want to forward the message to, and hitting the recall button again."

   Paraphrase: "Are you telling me _____

   _____

   _____

3. **Supervisor to employee:** "In order to qualify for community service hours, you need to fill out the paperwork in the career center, have your job supervisor sign off on the form that describes your work duties, and get your parents to sign off on the parental consent form."

   Paraphrase: "Let me get this straight. You want me to _____

   _____

   _____

4. **Coworker to coworker:** "Don't stand around looking like there's nothing to do! Look busy, or you'll get us all in trouble. You look like you're half asleep most of the time. Do you get any sleep at night?"

   Paraphrase: " _____

   _____

   _____

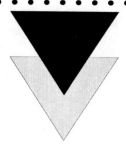

"Clear as a Bell?"

Paraphrasing Log

Bring back an example of how you used effective paraphrasing, either at home, school, or work. Answer the questions that follow.

Who was involved in this conversation?

How did you use paraphrasing effectively?

Would you be willing to role-play the conversation?

LESSON 17

Accepting Criticism

PURPOSE	**THE ABILITY TO ACCEPT CRITICISM FROM A SUPERVISOR, COWORKER, OR CUSTOMER IS CRUCIAL TO JOB SUCCESS.** In this lesson, students will learn reasonable methods of accepting criticism through practice and role-playing. They will be able to relate their knowledge of internal and external locus of control to effective strategies for dealing with critical feedback.
LEARNING OUTCOMES	◀ Students will recognize internal and external behavioral responses to situations involving criticism from a supervisor, coworker, or customer. ◀ Students will develop a method for accepting criticism based on a four-step "recipe."
REVIEW (5 MINUTES)	Students should use their "Clear As A Bell?" Paraphrasing Logs to discuss an example of paraphrasing that has occurred since the last lesson. If possible, encourage students to volunteer a role-playing scenario that accurately dramatizes the use of paraphrasing in a conversation.
REQUIRED MATERIALS	◀ "Clear as a Bell?" Paraphrasing Log from Lesson 16 ◀ Job Martyr Worksheet ◀ Recipe for Accepting Criticism overhead ◀ Negotiating the Storm (Vignettes) handout
LESSON 17 VOCABULARY	**HAVE STUDENTS REFER TO THEIR UNIT FOUR VOCABULARY LIST AS YOU INTRODUCE THE FOLLOWING VOCABULARY WORDS AND PHRASES.** **Accepting Criticism:** When a person is able to respond with a positive attitude to a supervisor, coworker, or customer who wants something done differently. Example: being able to smile while your editor tells you that a chapter needs to be rewritten for the twelfth time. **Feedback:** Information that is provided as a response to an action, event, or behavior that can be used to create improvement or change. Example: "Mike's boss provided him with feedback that allowed him to become the company's leading salesman." **Internal Response:** A response that reflects an internal locus of control (i.e., owning, responsibility, self-control). For example, an internal response to a demanding customer might be "I'm sorry you feel so badly about the delay; can I offer you something to drink?"

LESSON 17 VOCABULARY (CONTINUED)	**External Response:** A response that reflects an external locus of control (i.e., moaning, blaming, whining). For example, an external response to a demanding customer might be "I can't help it if we are shorthanded!"

DESCRIPTION OF THE ACTIVITY

ACTIVITY 17.1   JOB MARTYR (15 MINUTES)

This activity will introduce students to a Recipe for Accepting Criticism and will allow them to practice using this recipe with statements from a worksheet.

◀ **View** the overhead depicting the four-step Recipe for Accepting Criticism. Discuss this "recipe" with the students.

◀ **Hand out** the Job Martyr Worksheet with examples of typical worksite statements that are critical of an employee's actions or character. Spend time discussing these and other statements that create a feeling of defensiveness, embarrassment, or anger.

◀ **As a group**, apply the four-step recipe to the statements on the Job Martyr Worksheet. Each student should turn in a copy when you are done.

ACTIVITY 17.2   NEGOTIATING THE STORM (25 MINUTES)

This activity provides a role-play situation in which students can apply the four-step recipe for accepting criticism.

◀ **Divide** students into teams of four.

◀ **Hand out** the Negotiating the Storm workplace vignettes (at the end of this lesson) to be role-played by teams. Have two team members enact the vignettes showing little evidence of accepting criticism, and then have the other two team members use the four-step process to deal with criticism. First, have each pair role-play their situation just to the other members of their team.

◀ Next, **pick** several teams to present their role-plays to the entire class.

◀ As **each team** performs, provide constructive criticism to them. Reinforce those who present their scenarios to the entire class.

WRAP-UP/HOMEWORK

Emphasize to students that accepting criticism can be one of the most difficult parts of a job. For many people, it takes a great deal of effort to swallow their pride and utilize criticism to make themselves better employees. Encourage students to practice accepting criticism in as many situations as possible, including at home, with their peers, and on the job.

Name _____

Job Martyr

Worksheet

A "martyr" is a person who is willing to sacrifice his or her life (or, in this context, ego, pride, self-importance) for an important cause. Assuming that your job is the "cause," identify an internal response that will make you a "Job Martyr," an employee capable of accepting criticism from supervisors, coworkers, and customers.

Statements of Workplace Criticism:

1. **(Coworker)** "You always take your time going to and coming from the bathroom."
   Internal response: _____
   _____

2. **(Supervisor)** "You need to pay more attention to detail; you're costing us money!"
   Internal response: _____

3. **(Coworker)** "You said that you would be here at 6:30 am. It's 7:00 am."
   Internal response: _____

4. **(Customer)** "Why is it that you guys take so long to make a cup of coffee?"
   Internal response: _____
   _____

5. **(Supervisor)** "How many times do I need to explain this to you?"
   Internal response: _____
   _____

6. **(Customer)** "I don't care whether your boss is in a meeting, I need to talk with him."
   Internal response: _____
   _____

7. **(Coworker)** "You need to finish one task before you start another, no matter what."
   Internal response: _____
   _____

8. **(Supervisor)** "You look like you're half asleep."
   Internal response: _____

Recipe for
Accepting Criticism

LISTEN even if you don't like what you hear.

APOLOGIZE even if you are right.

ASK to explain your point of view.

ASK for suggestions to improve.

Negotiating the Storm

(Vignettes)

Each team should choose one of the short stories to role-play. Have two team members develop a role-play that reflects an external response by an employee to the work situation. The other two team members should use the Recipe for Accepting Criticism to design a role-play that demonstrates an internal response to the same situation. Each pair on your team should role-play their situation to the other two team members. Be prepared, however, to perform the role-play for the entire class.

Stories

Story One: Martin got a job as a busboy in a local restaurant. He was always working late, arriving home after midnight. He was getting angry that he could not work an earlier shift. It was beginning to have a negative influence on his schoolwork. Martin knew that his boss liked the work that he did, but he was unsure of how to change his hours. One evening his boss approached him concerning the fact that he had closed too early the night before. Martin had thought that the evening was so slow that nobody would mind if he closed early. He had a final exam the next day, anyway. If you were Martin what would you say?

Story Two: Lucy was hired as a teller at a local bank. She was asked to shadow the lead teller during her first week on the job. During the second week, Lucy was able to begin working directly with walk-in customers while being coached by the lead teller. In her third week she was expected to perform all transactions independently. During that week, her station came up $40 short. Her supervisor informed her that she would need to write a report describing to the best of her ability why the shortfall occurred. She didn't have the slightest idea why the problem occurred. What should Lucy do?

Story Three: Bill was working as an intern in a local print shop. His primary job was to package orders using shrink-wrap. He was then expected to prepare each order for shipment and call customers to inform them that their orders were ready for pick-up. During a busy week, Bill was unable to complete the packaging within the expected time lines. His supervisor received a scathing phone call from an unhappy customer who was displeased with the delay. When the supervisor confronted him, saying, "You need to stay on top of these deadlines or look for another job," Bill responded:

Story Four: Alice, a ninth grader, was refereeing basketball for the first time. Her partner had not arrived at the game prior to the start time. A parent volunteered to referee until her partner showed up. During the first quarter, the parent made some terrible calls that caused coaches and parents on the opposing team to begin screaming about the "crummy officiating." Alice felt that the game was getting out of control at the beginning of the next quarter. What would you do if you were Alice?

LESSON 18

Communicating With Power

PURPOSE	**THIS LESSON INTRODUCES STUDENTS TO A STYLE OF COMMUNICATION THAT WILL MAKE A DIFFERENCE IN HOW THEY ARE PERCEIVED IN THE WORKPLACE BY THEIR SUPERVISORS AND COWORKERS.** Students will "try on" three styles of communication—passive, aggressive, and assertive—and practice assertive communication, a style that exemplifies both strength and sensitivity and is the preferred communication mode for the workplace.
LEARNING OUTCOMES	◄ Students will recognize that an internal and an external locus of control influence the level of effective communication that occurs between people. ◄ Students will be able to demonstrate assertive communication as a self-advocacy technique.
REVIEW (5 MINUTES)	Ask students if they encountered any situations since the last lesson where they had to deal with criticism. Have students volunteer responses. Ask them: "Was the response internal or external?" Explain that today's lesson will be focused on using the same internal locus of control to develop assertive communication skills. Being able to accept criticism demonstrates one aspect of strong character, and the ability to be assertive with supervisors, coworkers, and customers is another valuable quality in the workplace.
REQUIRED MATERIALS	◄ Flip chart or white board ◄ Communication Styles overhead ◄ Paint Me Assertive Worksheet ◄ Stand Up for Yourself vignettes handout ◄ CBM Vocabulary Test #4

| LESSON 18 VOCABULARY | HAVE STUDENTS REFER TO THEIR UNIT 4 VOCABULARY LIST AS YOU INTRODUCE THE FOLLOWING VOCABULARY. |

Passive Communication Style: When a person gives the impression that everything is okay, even when it is not. Examples: not communicating directly with a coworker, avoiding eye contact, withholding feelings, and maintaining silence.

Aggressive Communication Style: When a person states how he or she feels and thinks without considering the feelings of others. Example: communicating with put-downs, sarcasm, and an air of superiority around coworkers.

Assertive Communication Style: When a person can communicate with confidence and sensitivity. Example: being able to refuse a request from a coworker without making them mad.

"I" messages: Statements containing "I" that are used to express opinions, thoughts, or feelings. These messages tend to represent statements of ownership from people who are acting with an internal locus of control. Example: "I have a hard time waiting in long lines and being around lots of people."

"You" messages: Statements containing "You" that are used to express opinions, thoughts, or feelings. These messages tend to represent statements of whining and blaming by people with an external locus of control. Example: "You shop entirely too much."

DESCRIPTION OF THE ACTIVITY

ACTIVITY 18.1 PAINT ME ASSERTIVE (15–20 MINUTES)

This activity will introduce students to the importance of "I" statements and will allow them to practice, as a large group, identifying communication styles.

◄ **Display** the Communication Styles overhead to help define passive, aggressive, and assertive styles of communication. Have students think of additional qualities associated with each style and list these on the board or flip chart.

◄ **Explain** how "I" messages and "You" messages impact a conversation between two people. Assertive statements generally contain "I" statements because they are not as threatening as "You" statements. "I" statements tend not to make the other person defensive.

◄ **Pass out** the Paint Me Assertive Worksheet and read examples. Have students decide as a group which style of communication is exemplified by each. Ask students to come up with assertive alternative statements. Each student should fill out a worksheet as the group works together.

ACTIVITY 18.2   STAND UP FOR YOURSELF (20 MINUTES)

This activity will allow students to practice generating assertive responses to workplace situations they might encounter.

◀ Form teams of five students each. Pass out the Stand Up for Yourself vignette sheet (located at the end of this lesson) that relates five workplace situations. Have each team member select a different situation and demonstrate an assertive response to other team members. After all team members have contributed responses, report examples of team responses to the large group.

CBM (10 MINUTES)

Hand out the CBM Vocabulary Test #4 to the students. Time them for seven minutes, then collect the tests. Use the results as a guide to student progress on vocabulary concepts.

WRAP-UP/HOMEWORK

Ask students to look for "assertive personalities" on TV, in videos, or in the newspaper before the next meeting. Explain that people with strong but sensitive characters are not easy to find.

Communication Styles

PASSIVE:
- "Try to ignore the problem. It will go away."
- Indirect; no eye contact. Wishy-washy.

AGGRESSIVE:
- "In your face!"
- "Whatever I say is right!"

ASSERTIVE:
- Firm, yet sensitive.
- "I understand that you are mad, but can we begin to make things better?"

Name _____

Paint Me Assertive Worksheet

In this exercise, identify each statement as passive, aggressive, or assertive. Decide on a way to make the statement assertive if it needs to be changed. Remember that assertive statements tend to be more internally driven and sound much less like blaming, whining, "You" statements. They also tend to reflect a measure of sensitivity to the person on the receiving end.

1. **Employee to Supervisor:** "You better notify me earlier if you want me to work on weekends."
   Aggressive

   Assertive example: "I would really be willing to work weekends if I knew you needed me to work a little sooner in advance."

2. **Employee to Supervisor:** "I think it's about time that I get a raise."

3. **Supervisor to Employee:** "You need to make arrangements to be at our meeting. If you can't make it, we'll look for someone else."

4. **Employee to Supervisor:** "Why is everyone else getting a promotion, and I never do?"

5. **Coworker to Coworker:** "Okay, I'll cover for you one more time. "

6. **Supervisor to Employee:** "You need to listen to what I am saying!"

7. **Employee to Supervisor:** "I'd rather not talk about it."

8. **Employee to Supervisor:** "I don't care to talk about it right now."

9. **Coworker to Coworker:** "Whatever you say is alright with me. I don't care, anyway."

10. **Coworker to Coworker:** "I get sick and tired of making all the decisions!"

Unit 4 ◀ Lesson 18

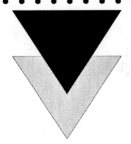

Stand Up for Yourself

Situation #1: Mary had been working as a troubleshooter in a software business for three days when a coworker told her, "When our supervisor isn't here, we usually take an extra break in the afternoon." This bothered her immediately. What could she say to the coworker in an assertive style?

Situation #2: John had received the employee of the month award as a financial analyst three times during the year. A coworker who had only been nominated for the award one time was given a promotion by his department supervisor. Although John was working in a different department, he felt that he deserved a promotion if his coworker was granted one. What should he say to his department supervisor?

Situation #3: Gloria was approached by a manager from a different insurance company and asked to come to work for a higher wage. She had been employed by her current company for two years and was on good terms with her staff and manager. Although she felt obligated to her present employer, she had some pressing financial needs at home. What could Gloria say to her present manager?

Situation #4: Rex was in the fourth hour of his first day on a job. The evening manager approached him with a can of chewing tobacco, and asked him if he wanted a "pinch." Rex did not chew, nor did he appreciate people who did. What could Rex say to his manager in an assertive style?

Situation #5: Amy was umpiring a softball game for 10-year-old girls. She made a call that was somewhat questionable, and a parent in the bleachers began yelling at her continually during the remaining innings. She did not feel that her call was wrong but didn't know how to respond to the parent. What could she do or say to the parent in an assertive style?

LESSON 19

Communicating With Self-Control

PURPOSE	**CONFLICT BETWEEN PEOPLE CAN BE HEALTHY. FOR AN ARGUMENT TO BE BENEFICIAL, PEOPLE MUST BE CAPABLE OF TURNING THE CORNER AND HEADING TOWARD "CONSTRUCTIVE COMMUNICATION."** This lesson allows students to experience communication from two perspectives: venting and empathy. Through a dynamic role-play they will practice "venting toward empathy" as they learn a self-control strategy that makes conflict healthier.
LEARNING OUTCOMES	◄ Students will demonstrate a communication strategy for maintaining self-control in stressful conversations.
REVIEW (5 MINUTES)	Operating from an internal locus of control allows people to avoid "going off." Ask students to recall Lessons 6 and 7, where they learned about self-control. Ask students if they have experienced any "firecrackers" since completing those lessons. Were they able to "cool off" and use affirmations to return to an internal locus of control? Explain that today's lesson should allow them to practice a strategy that can disarm the person throwing the "firecrackers."
REQUIRED MATERIALS	◄ Venting Toward Empathy Worksheet ◄ Chairs (4 chairs/team) ◄ Argument Cue Cards ◄ Observations form
LESSON 19 VOCABULARY	**HAVE STUDENTS REFER TO THEIR UNIT FOUR VOCABULARY LIST AS YOU INTRODUCE THE FOLLOWING VOCABULARY WORDS.** **Vent:** To get things "off one's chest." An expression of anger and frustration over a situation or behavior. For example: "Mr. Hicks, you make me sick the way you treat all of us during the holidays!" **Empathy:** To be able to see things from the other person's perspective. For example, "Mr. Hicks, I understand why the holidays are a tough time of year for you."

DESCRIPTION OF ACTIVITY

ACTIVITY 19.1 **VENTING TOWARD EMPATHY** (20 MINUTES)

Students will be able to translate venting statements into empathy statements as they complete this worksheet. This exercise should provide practice in "softening" the tone of communication with paraphrasing and "I" statements.

- ◄ **Divide** students into teams of four. Have each team appoint a recorder.

- ◄ **Hand out** a Venting Toward Empathy Worksheet to each team. Have teams work together on translating the "venting" statements into "empathy" statements.

- ◄ **Model** the first example. Explain to students that venting statements generally include many "firecrackers" and "You" statements. On the other hand, empathizing statements tend to use paraphrasing and "I" statements. Empathy requires statements that are open and nonthreatening.

- ◄ **Discuss** the responses as an entire class, after teams have completed their worksheets.

ACTIVITY 19.2 **TAKING IT TO A HIGHER LEVEL** (25 MINUTES)

Students will role-play a simulated argument between two opposing parties. They will practice "venting" their opinions in heated disagreement before being able to cooly "empathize" with the opposing side. Using chairs as props, students will practice elevating their communication skills by physically moving from chair #1 (venting) to chair #2 (empathy).

- ◄ **Using the same teams of four**, have students form pairs within each team.

- ◄ **Arrange** four chairs within teams so that two are opposite the other two.

- ◄ **Argument Cue Cards** are then drawn by each pair within the larger team to decide which side of the argument they will represent. For example, in Argument Cue Card #1, one student plays the math teacher, while the other student plays the student.

- ◄ **Model** the activity by seating a pair of students directly across from one another in the first two chairs. Have them read their Argument Cue Card to the class. Next, they should determine which side of the argument they will represent. Solicit venting statements from the class that might be appropriate. Move the pair into the empathy chairs. Ask students to volunteer statements that might qualify as empathy statements.

- ◄ **Clarify** that, when they are seated in chair #1, statements can be abrasive and emotional. When they are seated in chair #2, their statements must be softer and more open. If the communication continues to be aggressive when a person is seated in chair #2, they should physically move back to chair #1. **Remember:** Students *must* be in the chair that reflects the way they are communicating.

- ◂ **Emphasize** that venting statements contain "firecrackers" and lots of "You" statements, while empathy statements tend to contain more paraphrasing and "I" statements.

- ◂ **Each pair** will role-play their argument to the other two members of the larger team.

- ◂ **Observations forms** should be completed by the team members who are observing the role-play. When the role-plays are over, ask for examples from these forms. For example, ask students to name some of the venting words they heard.

Wrap-Up/Homework

Ask students if they see any difference between communicating with supervisors and customers versus coworkers. Stress the importance of moving more quickly from the venting chair to the empathy chair in situations involving customers and supervisors. Venting can cost a person their job or alienate a loyal customer if it fails to move toward empathy soon enough. Discuss how "cooling off" and "affirmations" might help a person move to "chair #2."

Venting Toward Empathy

Worksheet

Change the following venting statements to empathy statements. Remember that empathy statements attempt to experience or understand the other side of the argument. They tend to reflect paraphrasing and "I" statements.

Example:

Change *"You don't have the slightest idea of how to give decent directions!"*

To *"I seem to have a hard time following these directions. Should I ask more questions?"*

1. "You are late to everything that you ever attend!"

2. "Can't you do anything right the first time?"

3. "You are costing this company a lot of money because you don't care about your work!"

4. "I don't think you have the slightest idea of what you're talking about!"

5. "You never explain things enough for me to understand what I need to be doing."

6. "Why don't you go stick your nose in someone else's business?"

7. "You think you know everything! You're such a know-it-all!"

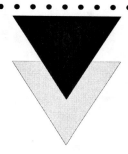

Argument Cue Cards

1.

Your math teacher has asked you to stay after school to talk about your failing grade. When you arrive at her office she says, *"You need to realize what a disappointment you've been in this class."*

You want to respond with, *"You do a lousy job of explaining things!"*

2.

Your science teacher tells you, *"If you spent less time at work and more time doing homework, you might graduate."*

You would like to respond with, *"Your class is a lot more boring than my job!"*

3.

Your employer has just denied you the opportunity to go home early so you can study for a final exam. He says, *"You high school kids need to learn what responsibility is all about."*

You want to respond with, *"I'll bet you never finished high school!"*

4.

A coworker approaches you after you have reported him for harassment and says, *"You didn't have to report me. If you can't take what's dished out, find another job!"*

You would prefer to respond with, *"Maybe you need to understand what a jerk you are!"*

Argument Cue Cards (continued)

5.

A coworker has arrived late to work for the third time this week. Every time this happens, your crew gets penalized by not qualifying for a production bonus.

You want to tell him, *"Why don't you start thinking about somebody other than yourself?"*

6.

Your supervisor is never around when you have a question during your first days on the job. You ask a coworker how to work the "banding" machine for cardboard. When your supervisor sees you, he says, *"You have no business operating that dangerous piece of machinery!"*

You want to approach the coworker and ask her, *"Why didn't you tell me that I shouldn't be operating that piece of equipment?"*

7.

You are working with a roofing crew, and your supervisor has given you the toughest job, shoveling gravel onto the conveyor belt. This is normally a two-person job.

You are exhausted by the afternoon break. At break, you want to tell him, *"You are not being fair to me!"*

8.

A coworker who is older than you keeps following you around and it makes you feel uncomfortable. It seems like he is never working when you are.

You finally say, *"Aren't you supposed to be working somewhere?"*

9.

A coworker was supposed to take your shift the night before and didn't show up. You got in trouble, because you didn't tell the boss. When you see the coworker you want to ask, *"Where were you last night? Do you know that I got in trouble?"*

The coworker responds with, *"I thought it was tonight."*

10.

One of your secretaries seems to be missing a lot of work. It seems like every time that you need to ask her for help, she's gone.

When you ask her to make travel arrangements with a local travel agency, she says, *"You'll need to have someone else do that. I have a doctor's appointment."*

11.

You are the supervisor of an instructional aide who is constantly observed chatting in the hallway, teacher's lounge, and library. You approach the aide by saying, *"What do you do around here, other than talk?"*

He responds by saying, *"What's wrong with talking?"*

12.

You are umpiring a softball game and one of the coaches is being really nasty to you. After you call one of his runners out at home, he comes off the bench and says, *"You're as blind as a bat!"*

You want to tell him, *"Save your compliments for somebody that cares."*

Argument Cue Cards (continued)

13.

You have been working for a logging operation where you must pay room and board out of your paycheck. All you ever get for breakfast is "burned pancakes." The company takes $6.00/day out for breakfast.

You approach your employer by asking, *"How many more days do I have to eat burned pancakes?"*

14.

A customer criticizes your work as a waitress by saying, *"You are the most unfriendly person who has ever served us!"*

You want to say, *"Why don't you go somewhere else then?"*

Observations

While students are observing the other members of their team role-play venting and empathy, use the following form to record information that can be discussed after the role-play.

How many words did you hear that sounded like venting words? List as many as possible:

Did the tone change when they moved to chair #2?

Describe how the conversation changed:

When evaluating the performance of the two participants in this role-play, what do you think they did well?

What could they have improved?

LESSON 20

Enthusiasm

PURPOSE	**THIS LESSON FOCUSES ON THE PERSONAL QUALITY OF ENTHUSIASM AND ITS IMPORTANCE IN SCHOOL AND THE WORKPLACE.** Students will learn that a strong internal locus of control is essential to being enthusiastic. They also will learn that optimism and positive thinking are necessary to sustain an enthusiastic attitude.
LEARNING OUTCOMES	◀ Students will be able to explain how optimism and "thinking positively" influence the level of enthusiasm demonstrated in various settings. ◀ Students will understand the connection between an internal locus of control and the personal quality of enthusiasm.
REVIEW (5 MINUTES)	Review the three styles of communication covered in Lesson 18. Discuss the differences between passive, aggressive, and assertive communication styles. Relate how the characters presented on television, in videos, and in the newspaper have demonstrated assertive communication styles. For example, read some letters from the editorial page of a newspaper that offer assertive styles of communication.
REQUIRED MATERIALS	◀ Editorial letters ◀ Flip chart or white board ◀ Enthusiasm overhead ◀ Life on the Bright Side overhead
LESSON 20 VOCABULARY	**HAVE STUDENTS REFER TO THEIR UNIT FOUR VOCABULARY LIST AS YOU INTRODUCE THE FOLLOWING VOCABULARY WORDS.** **Enthusiasm:** The measure of how much a person enjoys his or her work, and expresses that enjoyment appropriately to others. Example: encouraging coworkers to eat lunch together once a week. **Optimism:** An attitude that allows one to see the bright side in situations. Example: the ability to accept being laid off from a job because it provides a good opportunity to find a better one.

DESCRIPTION OF THE ACTIVITY:

ACTIVITY 20.1   A GLASS HALF FULL (15 MINUTES)

This activity will enable students to understand that enthusiasm is a product of the hope and optimism that is present in people who possess a strong internal locus of control.

‹ **Pair** students up with one another and have them generate a list of five qualities that define enthusiasm. After a few minutes, ask for examples. Record their ideas on the flip chart or white board. Next, have the same pairs of students come up with one example of enthusiasm that they have witnessed in the workplace or at school. With the entire class, ask students to volunteer three to five examples of workplace or school enthusiasm.

‹ **Display** the Enthusiasm overhead with quotes from employers describing the value of enthusiasm. Next, display the Life on the Bright Side overhead. Discuss how enthusiasm is easier to demonstrate if things are going well at home, at school, or on the job, yet, when things "turn sour," it is harder to maintain an enthusiastic attitude. The purpose of this assignment is to generate slogans that represent hope and optimism when things "go sour." Again, working in pairs, have teams generate two or three slogans similar to the examples on the Life on the Bright Side overhead.

ACTIVITY 20.2   LIFE ON THE BRIGHT SIDE (25–30 MINUTES)

This activity will allow students to demonstrate enthusiasm, optimism, and positive thinking via role-plays.

‹ **Form** teams of eight by having four existing pairs (the pairs from Activity 20.1) combine.

Within the larger team, have each pair choose one of their own slogans and prepare a short skit for the group demonstrating enthusiasm and optimism. After all teams have presented within their groups, ask each team of eight to nominate a skit to be presented to the entire class.

‹ **Discuss** the significance of maintaining a strong internal locus of control for being optimistic and enthusiastic. Explain that people who are able to "live on the bright side" tend to be people with solid internal control.

WRAP-UP/HOMEWORK

Explain to students that workplace enthusiasm is a strong indicator of a solid employee. Have them look for signs of enthusiasm as they go about their business in school and the community. Refer students to their Locus of Control Log (you might need to hand out more of these forms), and have them record three examples of enthusiasm or lack of enthusiasm that they observe. Rather than recording a locus of control event, simply record the act of enthusiasm. After recording the act, have students identify why it was internal. For example, an act of enthusiasm might be a coworker telling another coworker about a new program that will help them do their jobs better. This would be considered an internal act of responsibility and ownership.

Enthusiasm

"Just find me an employee who
can show up and be nice."

Ron Keebler, Photographer, The Oregon Gallery

"Leave your problems at home.
Be polite . . . even in spite of your feelings."

Sam Jenkins, Taco Time Manager

"Attitudes are the whole ballpark.
Don't think the work is for you . . .
It's for the customers."

June Jackson, Theater Owner

Life on the Bright Side

"When life gives you lemons, make lemonade.
(Just add sugar and water.)"

"Is your glass half empty or half full?"

"Tomorrow is the first day of the rest of your life."

"Look at the bright side of life."

LESSON 21

Peer Interviews Orientation

PURPOSE	**THIS ORIENTATION LESSON HELPS PREPARE STUDENTS FOR LESSONS 22, 23, AND 24.** The instructor, as well as some students, will model interviewing techniques through practice interviews. Students will learn: (a) how to rate other students on their interviewing skills and (b) what skills are most important to consider when interviewing for a job.
LEARNING OUTCOMES	◄ After observing sample interviews, students will be prepared to participate in mock interviews with their peers. ◄ Students will understand how to rate their peers' interviewing skills using a peer rating form.
REVIEW (15 MINUTES)	Review some of the acts of enthusiasm that students have gathered since the last class. Then ask students to take out the résumés they have prepared. Have them pair up and read each other's résumé and give feedback regarding necessary changes and/or improvements. Tell the students to bring their résumés to their peer interviews, which will be conducted in the following three lessons (Lessons 22, 23, and 24).
REQUIRED MATERIALS	◄ Job Interview Peer Rating Forms ◄ Sample Interview Questions overhead
LESSON 21 VOCABULARY	**PLEASE HAVE STUDENTS REFER TO THEIR UNIT FOUR VOCABULARY LIST AS YOU INTRODUCE THESE WORDS.** **Interviewer:** The person who conducts the job interview. For example, the manager of a restaurant might interview potential employees. **Interviewee:** The person who seeks the job and must answer questions in order to be evaluated by the interviewer. For example, a 17-year-old high school senior interviews for a job at a fast food restaurant. **Greeting:** The way an interviewee introduces himself or herself to an interviewer. For example, a firm handshake, eye contact, a smile, "Nice to meet you, _____ ," good posture, and telling the interviewer your name are aspects of a strong greeting.

DESCRIPTION OF ACTIVITY

ACTIVITY 21.1 **LEARNING THE QUESTIONS AND THE FORMS** (10 MINUTES)

This activity will prepare students to practice rating their peers and will orient them to the interview skills you want them to learn.

◄ Place a transparency of the Sample Interview Questions on the overhead or write the questions on the board.

◄ Review these questions with the students, asking them for ideas on good strategies for answering the questions.

◄ Hand out Job Interview Peer Rating Forms to every student.

◄ Explain the categories to the students, asking for their ideas about good strategies for achieving high scores. Refer to the vocabulary list as you explain these. Be sure they understand how to fill out the forms (4 is most skilled; 1 is least skilled).

ACTIVITY 21.2 **PRACTICING FOR THE INTERVIEWS** (30 MINUTES)

This activity will provide models for the students of what constitutes good and poor interviewing skills. Students will also be able to practice using the Peer Rating Forms. Each interview should take approximately five minutes.

◄ Ask for a volunteer to be the first interviewee. If no one volunteers, choose a student. Be sure to reinforce and praise those students who participate in the interviews. For the first one or two interviews, you should be the interviewer, to model appropriate interview behavior. However, emphasize that students will be interviewing other students over the next three lessons.

◄ Make sure the student enters the interviewing area in such a way that he or she can demonstrate his or her greeting skills.

◄ Ask as many of the questions from the Sample Interview Questions as you want.

◄ Have the other students individually rate the student's interviewing skills using the Peer Rating Forms.

◄ After the interview, evaluate the student's interview as a group, pointing out first what went well, and then asking for constructive criticism from the other students.

◄ Repeat this exercise for one or two more students, asking for one student to volunteer to be the interviewer at least one time.

◄ Clarify any questions or concerns the students have.

Wrap-Up/Homework

Tell students which day they will be interviewed. Remind students they should bring their completed résumés to class that day. Instruct them to think of jobs they eventually would like to hold. Have them place their name and the type of job they would like to interview for on a piece of paper and turn it in to you. Also, stress the importance of dressing appropriately for their interviews. Remind students of the importance of showing respect to each of their peers during the practice interviews.

 # Sample Interview Questions

Employer/Interviewer _____ Student Interviewee _____

EMPLOYERS!

You can modify these questions and/or create your own questions, but **please record the question that was substituted**. Make sure, however, that all of your questions are phrased in such a way that it is clear the questions are related to the job and not to the interviewee's personal life. It is illegal for employers to ask those types of questions.

1. What qualifications/experience do you have that make you believe you will be successful in this job?

2. How would you describe yourself as it relates to this job in one word?

3. How well do you work under pressure? Tell me about a situation in which you had to work or complete a task while under a lot of pressure.

4. What are your strengths as an employee?

5. What about yourself do you feel you need to work on in order to improve your skills as an employee?

6. In what type of environment are you most comfortable working? (For example, do you work better in structured environments with lots of rules or in laid-back environments?)

7. Do you have any questions for me about the interview process, the hiring process, or this job?

Job Interview
Peer Rating Forms

Your Name: _____

Interviewee: _____

On a Scale of 1–4, rate the interviewee on the following
(Circle your response—4 is very skilled; 1 is least skilled):

1. Greeting   1   2   3   4

2. Dress & Grooming   1   2   3   4

3. Ability to Answer Questions   1   2   3   4

4. Nonverbal Communication   1   2   3   4

5. Ability to Ask Questions   1   2   3   4

Total Score _____

Your Name: _____

Interviewee: _____

On a Scale of 1–4, rate the interviewee on the following
(Circle your response—4 is very skilled; 1 is least skilled):

1. Greeting   1   2   3   4

2. Dress & Grooming   1   2   3   4

3. Ability to Answer Questions   1   2   3   4

4. Nonverbal Communication   1   2   3   4

5. Ability to Ask Questions   1   2   3   4

Total Score _____

Your Name: _____

Interviewee: _____

On a Scale of 1–4, rate the interviewee on the following
(Circle your response—4 is very skilled; 1 is least skilled):

1. Greeting   1   2   3   4

2. Dress & Grooming   1   2   3   4

3. Ability to Answer Questions   1   2   3   4

4. Nonverbal Communication   1   2   3   4

5. Ability to Ask Questions   1   2   3   4

Total Score _____

Your Name: _____

Interviewee: _____

On a Scale of 1–4, rate the interviewee on the following
(Circle your response—4 is very skilled; 1 is least skilled):

1. Greeting   1   2   3   4

2. Dress & Grooming   1   2   3   4

3. Ability to Answer Questions   1   2   3   4

4. Nonverbal Communication   1   2   3   4

5. Ability to Ask Questions   1   2   3   4

Total Score _____

Lesson 22

Interviews With Peer Ratings (Part One)

PURPOSE	**THIS LESSON, ALONG WITH LESSONS 23 AND 24, CONSTITUTE A CULMINATION ACTIVITY FOR UNIT FOUR.** Using what they learned in previous lessons—especially Lesson 21—the students will each have a turn to be an interviewer and an interviewee in a mock job interview. All students will use Peer Rating Forms to give feedback to their peers regarding their interviewing skills.
LEARNING OUTCOMES	◄ By participating in interviews in front of the class, students will demonstrate they have learned the importance of specific interviewing skills, including their (a) greeting, (b) dress and grooming, (c) ability to answer questions, (d) nonverbal communication, and (e) ability to ask questions. ◄ Students will feel more confident interviewing for "jobs."
REVIEW (5 MINUTES)	Hand out the Peer Rating Forms to the students and quickly review each of the categories. Clarify any questions the students have about the interviews.
REQUIRED MATERIALS	◄ Peer Rating Forms (see Lesson 21) ◄ Sample Interview Questions (see Lesson 21) ◄ Two chairs and a table (for the interviewers and interviewees)
LESSON 22 VOCABULARY	There is no new vocabulary for this lesson.

DESCRIPTION OF ACTIVITY

ACTIVITY 22.1   GETTING DOWN TO BUSINESS (45 MINUTES)

This mock interviewing activity will give students the chance to experience what it feels like to be interviewed and will allow them to practice their interviewing skills in front of and with their peers.

◄ Prior to this lesson, you should have created a list of those students who will be interviewers and those students who will be interviewees in Lessons 22, 23, and 24.

◄ Prior to this lesson, you should decide how you want to grade or score your students for this activity. Ideas for grading include: (a) taking the average of the scores on the Peer Rating Forms; (b) taking the average of the Peer Rating Forms and your rating of the student; and (c) using your rating as the sole basis for the student's actual grade.

Whichever way of grading you choose, it is important that each student receive feedback from both you *and* his or her peers.

◄ Remind students to be respectful of one another during the mock interviews and to fill out a Peer Rating Form for each student.

◄ Begin by having the first student interviewer and interviewee come to the front of the classroom. Two chairs (and a table, if you wish) should be placed where everyone in the class can see them.

◄ Proceed with all of the interviews for day one. Reinforce students for their participation. You probably will not have time to provide much immediate feedback to each student following his or her interview. However, as mentioned before, be sure to provide both peer and teacher feedback, perhaps by giving each student copies of the completed Peer Rating Forms.

WRAP-UP/HOMEWORK

Briefly comment on how the interviews looked today. Again, reinforce the students for their participation. Getting up in front of the class to be evaluated by peers can be quite difficult for students. They need to feel comfortable and assured that they will not be rejected or made fun of by others in the class.

LESSON 23

Interviews With Peer Ratings (Part Two)

PURPOSE	This lesson is a continuation of the interviewing activity that began in Lesson 22. Please refer to that lesson for Learning Outcomes, Required Materials, and Description of Activity.
REVIEW	Hand out the Peer Rating Forms to the students and review the categories as needed. Answer any questions that students have before beginning the interview process for the day.
ADDITIONAL REQUIRED MATERIALS	CBM Vocabulary Test #5

DESCRIPTION OF ACTIVITY

ACTIVITY 23.1 GETTING DOWN TO BUSINESS (40 MINUTES)

Please refer to Lesson 22 and continue the interview process you began during that lesson. Today is the second of three days devoted to this particular activity. Be sure to monitor the time for each interview.

CBM (10 MINUTES)

Hand out the CBM Vocabulary Test #5 to the students. Time them for seven minutes, then collect their tests. Use the CBM as a guide to student progress with vocabulary concepts.

WRAP-UP/HOMEWORK

Briefly comment on how the interviews looked today. Reinforce the students for their participation, and review any interviewing skills as necessary.

LESSON 24

Interviews With Peer Ratings
(Part Three)

PURPOSE	This lesson is the final day of the interviewing activity that began in Lesson 22. Please refer to that lesson for Learning Outcomes, Required Materials, and Description of Activity.
REVIEW	Hand out the Peer Rating Forms to the students and review the categories as needed. Answer any questions the students have before beginning the interview process for the day.
ADDITIONAL REQUIRED MATERIALS	◄ Unit 4 Mastery Vocabulary Test

DESCRIPTION OF ACTIVITY

ACTIVITY 24.1 GETTING DOWN TO BUSINESS (45–50 MINUTES)

Please refer to Lesson 22, and continue the interview process you began during that lesson. Today is the third of three days devoted to this particular activity. You should complete all interviews today.

MASTERY TEST (5 MINUTES)

Give students the Unit 4 Mastery Vocabulary test and time them for five minutes.

WRAP-UP/HOMEWORK

After students have participated in these practice interviews it is an ideal time to invite employers from the community to participate in a mock interview event at the school. The inclusion of this complementary activity lends an added sense of reality to the interview process.

UNIT

5

LESSONS 25–33

PROBLEM SOLVING

LESSON 25

How Do I Solve the Problem?

PURPOSE	THIS LESSON INTRODUCES THE CONCEPT OF PROBLEM SOLVING AND ALLOWS STUDENTS TO PRACTICE SOLVING PROBLEMS COLLECTIVELY AND INDIVIDUALLY.
	This lesson provides students with a technique, called RADD, which they can use to solve any problem they encounter in the workplace.
COMPLEMENTARY ACTIVITIES	At some point in Unit Five, schedule time for the job shadow or industry tour activity suggested in Table 3 of the Instructor's Guide.
LEARNING OUTCOMES	◂ Students will generate a list of problem-solving steps that reflect their collective understanding of the problem-solving process.
	◂ Students will demonstrate effective problem solving, utilizing the RADD process to resolve a workplace situation involving dependability.
PROBLEM-SOLVING PRE-TEST (10 MINUTES)	Hand out the Problem-Solving Pre-Test, and ask students to complete the questions as you read them out loud. Make sure that every student marks an answer to each question in the appropriate space.
REQUIRED MATERIALS	◂ White board/chalkboard or flip chart
	◂ RADD Worksheet
	◂ Problem-Solving Pre-Test
	◂ Got a Problem? Worksheet
	◂ RADD Vignette #1
	◂ Unit Five Vocabulary List
LESSON 25 VOCABULARY	HAND OUT THE UNIT FIVE VOCABULARY LIST AND HAVE THE STUDENTS REFER TO THAT LIST AS YOU INTRODUCE THE FOLLOWING VOCABULARY WORDS.
	Problem: Any time a difficult situation occurs where there is no clear solution. For example, a flat tire happens on the way to work.
	Outcome: What needs to be accomplished by solving the problem. For example, what is the most important thing that needs to happen now that the tire is flat?
	Alternatives: Potential solutions to solving the problem. Examples: call work; start walking; call emergency road service; change the tire.
	Dependability: The measure of how much a person can be relied upon by coworkers and supervisors to perform work-related tasks.

Description of Activity

Activity 25.1 You Gotta Problem? (15–20 minutes)

This activity will introduce students to the RADD problem-solving technique by using a real-life dilemma/problem that has occurred in your life.

- ◄ **Present** students with a dilemma/problem that has occurred in your experiences as an employee, friend, family member, etc.

- ◄ **Ask** students to list the steps they would use to solve the problem.

- ◄ **Record** the steps on the board or on a flip chart.

- ◄ **Hand out** the RADD Worksheet and present the RADD process for problem solving by utilizing the RADD steps. Compare these steps to the ones they generated.

- ◄ **Walk** through the dilemma/problem that you presented using the RADD Worksheet.

- ◄ **Have students record** their ideas on their worksheets.

- ◄ **Share** ideas about solving the problem. Tell them how you solved the problem.

Activity 25.2 A Dependability Problem (20 minutes)

This activity will allow students to utilize the RADD technique with another problem. This is a problem involving dependability that could occur on the job.

- ◄ **Hand out** RADD Vignette #1 and another RADD Worksheet. Have students read about the problem encountered by the worker in the story. You may want to read the story aloud as a group.

- ◄ **Define** *Dependability* and what it means as an outcome of problem solving.

- ◄ **Have students record** their ideas about solving the problem on the RADD Worksheet.

- ◄ **Discuss** the ideas that were generated within each of the RADD areas.

Wrap-Up/Homework

Discuss with students how the manner in which they solved the problem may have had a lot to do with the way an employer might assess their level of dependability. Ask students to bring back a problem/dilemma from work, school, or family that occurs during the next few days. Have them record the problem on the Got a Problem? Worksheet and ask them to be prepared to share that information with the class.

Name _____

RADD Worksheet

RECOGNIZE the problem from all angles . . .

1. What do you want to accomplish/What is the desired outcome (e.g., dependability)?

2. What are all the things that are making it difficult to achieve the desired outcome?

ALTERNATIVES need to be generated . . . (at least 3)

1.

2.

3.

4.

5.

DECIDE on an alternative (or two) that makes the most sense.

DETERMINE if it was the right one . . .Try another alternative?

Name _____

Got a Problem?

Worksheet

Briefly describe your problem.

What is the desired outcome? What do you want to accomplish?

RADD

Vignette #1: Dependability

Situation:

Michelle got a new job as a waitress. On a Friday night, during the first week of employment, the boss told her that she had to help close up the restaurant.

Michelle did not want to help because she had a date, but her boss seemed very insistent that she work late.

Consider that . . .

Michelle is a seventeen-year-old who is currently a senior in high school. She is working twenty hours a week at the restaurant. Michelle has never worked before, and her sister was responsible for helping her get this job. She has never had a steady boyfriend, and this will be her third date. They are supposed to go to the 8:00 p.m. movie, and the restaurant closes at 8:00 p.m. She will be closing with the assistant manager, and this will be her first opportunity to do so.

Michelle's boss is a nice guy. He owns the restaurant. He hired Michelle on the recommendation of her sister, who worked for him before she enrolled full time at the community college. He is a family man and has two teenage children who are 13 and 16 years of age. He needs some time for them and has chosen to leave the restaurant early this evening to attend the high school football game. He is shorthanded tonight and feels like this will be a good test of Michelle's ability to make decisions that reflect how much she values her job.

Use your RADD Worksheet to problem solve Michelle's situation.

Problem-Solving Pre-Test

Becky has been working at the local college entering data for the admissions department. She has developed her skills in using many computer applications. The college has been so impressed with her that they have allowed her to work at home entering data. She has been given a modem and access to the Internet so that she has more capability to do work from home, but she is warned that the equipment is only for work and not for other, personal, use.

Becky has a younger brother who loves to surf the Internet on the family computer. On a day when the family computer was being used by his father, Becky's brother asks her if he can use her computer to access only his e-mail; he assures her that he will not do anything else on her computer because he knows she could get into trouble if he spent time using the computer for anything other than work-related tasks. She allows him to use her computer for an hour.

A week later, Becky receives a letter from the college computing center informing her that her computer privileges are being revoked because her activity account indicates that she has utilized her home computer for purchasing clothes on the Internet. Becky can't believe the accusation, but then she recalls allowing her brother to use her computer a week earlier.

Questions (Read out loud to the students; be sure that each student marks an answer for each question)

Please rate each of the following statements on the following scale:

> **3** – The statement is exactly in line with your impression from the scenario that was just read
> **2** – The statement is somewhat in line with your impression from the scenario that was just read
> **1** – The statement is not at all in line with your impression from the scenario that was just read

So, if the statement I read is exactly consistent with what you believe to be true from this scenario, mark your answer with a 3. If the statement I read is somewhat consistent with what you believe to be true from this scenario, mark your answer with a 2. If the statement I read is not at all consistent with what you believe to be true from this scenario, mark your answer with a 1.

RECOGNIZE

1. _____ Becky was told not to use the work computer for personal reasons.

2. _____ The situation is completely unfair because Becky did not use her computer for personal reasons.

3. _____ Becky's brother probably used the computer to purchase clothes.

4. _____ Becky is completely at fault for the situation—it was, after all, her computer.

5. _____ Becky's brother didn't know that by using the computer in the way he did, he would get her into trouble.

6. _____ Becky's father is to blame for the situation because he was tying up the home computer in the first place.

Ok, now I am going to provide some alternatives that Becky could do on the job in response to this problem. I want you to rate each of these statements on the following scale:

> **3** – The alternative is very effective in addressing the problem.
> **2** – The alternative is somewhat effective in addressing the problem.
> **1** – The alternative is not at all effective in addressing the problem.

So, if you think an alternative will be effective in addressing the problem, mark your answer with a 3. If you think the alternative would be somewhat effective in addressing the problem, mark your answer with a 2. If you think the alternative will be ineffective in addressing the problem, mark your answer with a 1.

ALTERNATIVES

7. _____ Becky should confront her brother and scream at him about the situation.

8 _____ Becky should lie to her boss at work and say that there was a mistake in the billing.

9. _____ There is nothing she can do, she should just ignore the situation and go to work without saying or doing anything.

10. _____ Becky should talk with her brother and have him go with her to the boss to sort out the whole situation.

11. _____ Becky should have her brother go to her boss on his own to confess about the problem.

12. _____ Becky should quit the job to avoid any further embarrassment..

13. _____ Becky should just level with her boss and ask for a second chance.

In this section I want you to determine the effectiveness of choosing each of the following alternatives as a plan of action.

So, if you think an alternative will be effective as a plan of action, mark your answer with a 3. If you think the alternative would be somewhat effective in addressing the problem, mark your answer with a 2. If you think the alternative will be ineffective in addressing the problem, mark your answer with a 1.

DECIDE AND DETERMINE

14. _____ Quit the job.

15. _____ Level with the boss and ask for a second chance.

16. _____ Ignore the situation and go on to work without saying or doing anything.

17. _____ Confront your brother and scream at him.

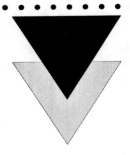

Agreed-Upon Ratings for Problem Solving Vignette

Pre-Test (Becky)

Lesson	1	2	3	4	5	6	7	8	9	10	11	12	13	14	15	16	17
Answer	3	1	3	3	1	1	1	1	1	3	1	1	3	1	3	2	1

LESSON **26**

Let's Solve Some of Our Own Problems

PURPOSE	THIS LESSON IS DESIGNED TO REINFORCE THE **RADD** TECHNIQUE OF PROBLEM SOLVING BY FOCUSING ON SITUATIONS STUDENTS HAVE SEEN OR PERSONALLY EXPERIENCED ON THE JOB, AT HOME, OR IN SCHOOL.
	Students will problem solve these situations collectively using the RADD approach. During this lesson, students will also get a chance to demonstrate their ability to problem solve a worksite situation as an assessment of their level of understanding.
LEARNING OUTCOMES	◄ Students will demonstrate collective problem solving skills utilizing the RADD technique on problems they self-report from work, home, or school.
	◄ Students will be able to demonstrate effective problem solving utilizing the RADD technique as they resolve an assigned problem.
REVIEW (5 MINUTES)	Ask students to help explain the RADD technique of problem solving. Write their responses on the board or on a flip chart. Have students volunteer to share some examples of problems that they have reported on the Got a Problem? Worksheet. Do not use the RADD technique on their self-reported problems at this time.
REQUIRED MATERIALS	◄ White board or flip chart ◄ RADD Worksheet (see Lesson 25) ◄ Fueling the Problem Vignette ◄ Got a Problem? Worksheet (see Lesson 25)
LESSON 26 VOCABULARY	There is no new vocabulary for this lesson.

DESCRIPTION OF ACTIVITY

ACTIVITY 26.1 LET'S HEAR FROM YOU GUYS (20–25 MINUTES)

This activity will allow students to collectively experience solving problems that have occurred in their lives.

- ◄ **Write the RADD** steps on the board (these steps should mirror the RADD Worksheet).

- ◄ **Ask** for a volunteer to share a problem that has been recorded on their Got A Problem? Worksheet.

- ◄ **Share and record** ideas about solving the problem using the RADD steps on the board.

- ◄ **Repeat** this process for one or two more problems that are volunteered by other students.

- ◄ **Reinforce** students for volunteering.

ACTIVITY 26.2 FUELING THE PROBLEM (20 MINUTES)

This activity will allow students to individually demonstrate in writing their knowledge of the RADD problem-solving strategy.

- ◄ **Hand out** the Fueling the Problem Vignette and a RADD Worksheet. Read the vignette with/to the group.

- ◄ **Assign** students the task of solving the problem from the vignette using the RADD Worksheet. Each student should complete the worksheet independently to indicate how well the student understands RADD.

- ◄ **Have students hand in** their RADD Worksheets, then discuss their problem-solving strategies as a large group.

WRAP-UP/HOMEWORK

Inform students that their responses to the Fueling the Problem Vignette will demonstrate a measure of their problem-solving ability. Offer incentives to students who are willing to bring back another completed Got a Problem? Worksheet with an accompanying RADD Worksheet on a problem that arises at home, work, or school.

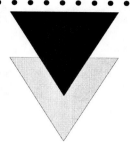

Fueling the Problem

Vignette

Situation:

Wayne's teacher found a job for him working at the Portland International Airport as part of the maintenance/support staff in the fueling department. His job consisted mainly of cleaning trucks and equipment used in fueling jet planes. He worked in this position for two summers and was well known by his coworkers. In fact, Wayne was asked to stay on after the summer of his senior year and work in a full-time position. An opening on the fueling crew developed during the summer, and Wayne would actually be responsible for fueling planes for cross-country trips across the United States. Wayne accepted the job enthusiastically and began a month-long training program where he would be taught safety and fueling procedures that were required by the Federal Aviation Administration (FAA). During the training, Wayne found it increasingly difficult to understand the math associated with converting volume to weight for jet fuel. The fueling crew was responsible for calculating the weight of the fuel being pumped into the wings of the jet liners as gallons of fluid. Wayne was feeling really anxious about the possibility of making a mistake in his conversions and possibly risking the lives of passengers and crew on the airliners that he would be responsible for supporting.

He was afraid that he might jeopardize his position if he let his supervisor know about his anxiety. Wayne realized that he would be making two dollars an hour more on this job and also be eligible for medical and sick leave benefits. He was confident that with the right assistance he could do what the job required, but he didn't know how to proceed with solving his problem.

Consider that . . .

Wayne graduated from high school with a standard diploma but was supported in math through a resource room in the Special Education department. His performance in school was only affected by his learning disability in processing numbers. He did fine in all of his other courses throughout his four years at the high school.

Wayne's supervisor hired him at the request of his teacher, who was also the varsity football coach at the high school. Wayne's teacher/coach never mentioned his disability to his supervisor because he didn't want to share confidential information about Wayne if it wasn't necessary.

Over the past two summers, Wayne has received glowing evaluations for his work. His latest promotion has everyone excited about his new responsibilities and full-time status.

Use your RADD Worksheet to problem solve Wayne's situation.

LESSON 27

Dependability

PURPOSE	**DEPENDABILITY IS THE PERSONAL QUALITY RATED AS A TOP PRIORITY BY EMPLOYERS NATIONWIDE, BUT HOW DO WE TEACH DEPENDABILITY? USING RADD, THIS LESSON ATTEMPTS TO LINK STUDENTS' PROBLEM-SOLVING SKILLS WITH THE CONCEPT OF DEPENDABILITY.**
	Students will realize that the outcome of their problem solving is to look and act dependable in the workplace. Students should also recognize that responding to problems from an internal locus of control will improve the likelihood of being dependable.
LEARNING OUTCOMES	◄ Students will evaluate problems on the job associated with dependability from an internal locus of control perspective. ◄ Students will make decisions using RADD that demonstrate dependability in the workplace.
REVIEW (5 MINUTES)	Ask students to volunteer some examples of problems that they have reported on their Got a Problem? and RADD Worksheets. Offer rewards to all students who have written examples of problems encountered and solved. Tell students that today they will be solving problems focused on looking and acting dependable.
REQUIRED MATERIALS	◄ White board or flip chart ◄ RADD Worksheet (see Lesson 25) ◄ Paint Me Dependable Worksheet ◄ Are You Dependable? Vignettes
LESSON 27 VOCABULARY	**HAVE STUDENTS REFER TO THEIR UNIT FIVE VOCABULARY LIST AS YOU INTRODUCE THE FOLLOWING VOCABULARY.** **Responsibility:** A sense or feeling of ownership that leads one to act in a dependable manner. Example: the feeling one might have when one is in charge of opening and closing at a restaurant. **Punctuality:** Another way of saying "on time." Punctuality means showing up to work, meetings, and events before they begin.

DESCRIPTION OF ACTIVITY

ACTIVITY 27.1 PAINT ME DEPENDABLE (20 MINUTES)

This activity will allow students to collectively brainstorm the most important facets of dependability in the workplace.

- ◄ **Discuss** with students how dependability may not be something that is evident in every part of their lives. Ask when they feel most dependable. Write their responses on the white board or flip chart.

- ◄ **Determine** those times when students do not act dependably. Record their responses on the board. Try to highlight the determining factor(s) encouraging dependability (e.g., "When I am in a position of responsibility").

- ◄ **Hand out** the Paint Me Dependable Worksheet. Ask students to respond to each situation by writing a phrase or short sentence suggesting how a dependable person would react.

ACTIVITY 27.2 ARE YOU DEPENDABLE? (20–25 MINUTES)

This activity incorporates the RADD process in solving problems from a selection of vignettes that test dependability. These selections should allow students to think about responsible decision making and its association with an internal locus of control.

- ◄ **Hand out** to each student the Are You Dependable? Vignettes and a RADD Worksheet for each vignette (or they can write on their own paper).

- ◄ **Explain** to students that the vignettes have been developed to test their problem-solving ability about acting dependably at school and in the workplace. Remind them of the importance of responding to situations with an internal locus of control. Tell them they may need to take the vignettes and worksheets home as their homework if they don't complete them by the end of class. This will serve as their homework.

- ◄ **Reinforce** those students who work diligently for the remainder of the period.

WRAP-UP/HOMEWORK

Emphasize to students the value of responding to any work situation from an internal locus of control. Most problems on the job occur when people react from an external locus of control. Inform students that the way in which they problem solve the four Are You Dependable? vignettes will test their ability to keep an internal focus. Tell them that they will be placed on teams for lessons 32 and 33, when each team will be responsible for using the RADD technique on one of the vignettes from this lesson or the next lesson (Lesson 28).

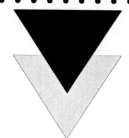

Name _____

Paint Me Dependable

Worksheet

What would a dependable person do? Answer each situation with a short phrase.

1. On the way to work, you get in an accident.

2. A coworker offers to give you a ride home, but accepting means that you will be leaving five minutes early.

3. Your mother wants you to babysit during the morning instead of going to your job.

4. You wake up with a headache and sore throat and feel like not going to work.

5. You are asked to close the restaurant that evening, when you have a final exam in the morning.

6. You know that you will be 10 minutes late to work because you overslept.

7. You are at the first of two morning meetings, and it looks like the first meeting will run over into the next.

8. One of your teachers wants to talk to you after school, which means you will be late for work.

　　© The State of Oregon. User has permission to copy this page for classroom use.

Are You Dependable?

Vignettes

Students should respond to the four vignettes using their RADD worksheets. They should be reminded that dependability is the desired outcome for each situation.

Vignette #1

Before Bob was hired for his current job as a bank teller at the local credit union, he and his fiancée had set a marriage date and planned a honeymoon. During the interview, Bob was not sure that he wanted to mention his upcoming marriage because it might jeopardize his chances of getting the job. Since being hired, he has questioned when the appropriate moment might be to ask his supervisor for the two weeks necessary to get married and go to Hawaii.

During his month on the job, Bob has been trained by the lead teller and has finally progressed to a level of competency where he no longer needs individual attention. This is vacation season for most of his coworkers, but he must wait a year before getting a paid vacation. He knows that time off for the wedding is going to be a sacrifice financially, but the wedding and honeymoon are being financed by the families. His fiancée has been able to arrange for time off at her job. Now he must figure out how to do the same. The wedding is in one month.

Vignette #2

Becky has been a teacher's aide in the school district for two years. She is growing tired of her role in the classroom, because it seems that all she does is run the copy machine and do busy work for the teachers in the English department. Becky wants more of a connection to the students. She would like to finish her education and become a teacher. This means enrolling in a two-year program offered by the university in her community.

After talking with her college advisor it appears that she will be able to keep her job as an aide, but she must negotiate her afternoon schedule around courses offered on campus. She hasn't yet mentioned anything to the teacher who is her supervisor. Becky is financially dependent on her current job and doesn't want to accumulate additional student loans in finishing her education. Her classes for the first session will involve missing an hour and a half of work, three times a week. Before she speaks with her supervisor Becky needs to consider her options.

Vignette #3

Peggy was hired to work in maintenance with the city parks department. Her role has varied over the three weeks that she has worked in the field. Lately, Peggy has been placed in charge of watering the athletic fields. Her hours have been flexible because the watering needs to occur during the evenings and early mornings. She generally turns the sprinklers on at 9:00 p.m. after having dinner with her family. Peggy is also responsible for early morning watering on another set of fields at 5:30 a.m. before reporting to the maintenance office.

One Friday, Peggy had an opportunity to go out of town on a camping trip with her family. She needed to make arrangements with a coworker to cover her watering responsibilities. Because Saturday was not a work day for the maintenance department, the job would involve starting the Friday evening and Saturday morning sprinklers. Rick, the coworker she convinced to fill in for her, said he would take care of everything. He told her there was no reason to even mention it to their supervisor.

When Peggy returned to work on Monday, she was told by another coworker that the fields did not get watered over the weekend. After approaching Rick, he simply stated that he had a fight with his girlfriend and, instead of watering the fields on Friday night, took care of all of them on Saturday. Peggy wasn't sure what to do.

Vignette #4

Ron was hired to work at a local feed and seed. He was given a job in the warehouse where he loaded grain sacks and hay bales into the vehicles of customers. The work was exhausting. Ron needed every break that he was given, and there were only three in a full day on the job. During his afternoon break he was so tired from the work of the day and the heat that he fell asleep and woke up fifteen minutes too late. He had been working for three weeks, and was developing a good record of being on time. He knew that punctuality was valued by his supervisor, but this incident would cost him. Ron wasn't sure what to do to look dependable.

LESSON 28

Honor Role

PURPOSE	**THIS LESSON FOCUSES ON ANOTHER PERSONAL QUALITY THAT IS VITAL TO SUCCESS IN THE WORKPLACE: HONESTY.** There is no quicker way to get fired from a job than to act in a dishonest manner. By using RADD, this lesson attempts to develop students' problem-solving skills associated with honesty. Students will also recognize that responding to problems from an internal locus of control should improve the likelihood of making honest decisions.
LEARNING OUTCOMES	◀ Students will evaluate problems associated with honesty on the job from an internal locus of control. ◀ Students will make decisions using RADD that demonstrate honesty in the workplace.
REVIEW (5 MINUTES)	Before having students hand in the four vignettes that were assigned in Lesson 27, ask them to volunteer information recorded on their RADD Worksheets. Ask students if they feel the problems were solved best from an internal or external locus of control. Tell students that today they will be solving problems focusing on honesty.
REQUIRED MATERIALS	◀ White board or flip chart ◀ RADD Worksheet (see Lesson 25) ◀ Honor Role Worksheet ◀ Honesty Vignettes
LESSON 28 VOCABULARY	**HAVE STUDENTS REFER TO THE UNIT FIVE VOCABULARY LIST AS YOU INTRODUCE THE FOLLOWING VOCABULARY WORDS.** **Honesty:** A personal quality that a person possesses that creates a strong sense of faith and trust in their character. For example, people who possess honesty are not accused of stealing when cash disappears from the register. **Exaggeration:** Stretching the truth to make a favorable impression. For example, someone might stretch the truth by telling the supervisor he or she isn't feeling well so he or she can go home early. The person may only have a headache but really want to get home to deal with a needy family member.

DESCRIPTION OF ACTIVITY

ACTIVITY 28.1 HONOR ROLE (20 MINUTES)

This activity allows students to decide on an honest or dishonest response to situations. Their responses should reflect both an internal and external perspective.

◄ **Discuss** with students how honesty can be dependent upon a person's locus of control. Explain that blaming, whining, making excuses, and exaggerating are external responses that can be elevated into lies and dishonest behavior. On the other hand, an internal locus of control allows people to admit mistakes, apologize, and move on when things go wrong.

◄ **Ask** students if they have encountered any situations where dishonesty cost someone his job. How about her grade in a class? His freedom and rights at home?

◄ **Hand out** the Honor Role Worksheet. Use the worksheet as an opportunity to discuss internal and external versions of honestly and dishonestly responding to workplace problems. Solicit additional examples that students might relate from their work, home, and school experiences.

ACTIVITY 28.2 HONESTY VIGNETTES (25 MINUTES)

This activity incorporates the RADD process in solving problems from a selection of vignettes that test honesty. These selections should allow students to think about responsible decision making and its association with an internal locus of control.

◄ **Pair students** up in teams of two. **Hand out** the Honesty Vignettes and RADD Worksheets to each team member.

◄ **Explain** to students that the vignettes have been developed to test their problem-solving ability related to the workplace. Remind them of the importance of responding to situations with an internal locus of control. Tell them they may need to take the vignettes and worksheets home if they don't complete them by the end of class. This will serve as their homework.

◄ Students should work together as a team to complete their individual worksheets. Reinforce those students who work diligently for the remainder of the period.

WRAP-UP/HOMEWORK

Inform students that the way in which they problem solve the four Honesty vignettes will test their ability to approach problems from an internal locus of control. Tell them that they will be placed on teams for lessons 32 and 33, when each team will be responsible for using the RADD technique on one of the vignettes from this lesson or the previous lesson (Lesson 27).

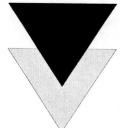

Name _____

Honor Role
Worksheet

The following situations may be resolved honestly or dishonestly. Provide an honest and a dishonest example of how the situation might be handled. Please respond with proper examples of exaggeration and confession when indicated.

1. At closing, you discover that your cash register contains $50.00 too much.
   Honest:

   Dishonest:

2. Your supervisor asks you to work overtime, but you have a date.
   Honest: (confess)

   Dishonest: (exaggeration)

3. You want to leave early because it is hot in the office. You are the only one there.
   Honest:

   Dishonest:

4. The machine that you are operating breaks down as your shift ends. You have a date.
   Honest:

   Dishonest:

5. You lack 10 hours of work experience to get your ½ credit for a class. This is your last timecard.
   Honest:

   Dishonest:

6. A coworker asks you to cover his last half hour so he can leave early. Your supervisor asks you where the coworker is.
   Honest: (confess)

   Dishonest: (exaggeration)

Honesty Vignettes

Students should respond to the four vignettes using their RADD Worksheets. They should be reminded that honesty is the desired outcome for each situation.

Vignette #1

Richard works for a local produce company during the summer of his senior year. He will be attending college in the fall and is working so that he can afford the expense of tuition and room and board. His job consists of delivering fruit and vegetables to numerous grocery stores throughout the community. It is common practice for employees of the company to snack on the fruit while it is being loaded at the warehouse. There is a policy that no fruit should be consumed once the deliveries are being made. The reason for this is that the customers might feel that they are getting cheated in quantity if the delivery man is eating their purchased items. After working most of the morning, Richard turned the corner too sharply in the delivery truck and spilled two crates of tomatoes on the bed of the truck. Many of the tomatoes were bruised, yet most were in good shape. Richard began picking up the tomatoes realizing that he could rearrange things so the crates would look undamaged. What would you do?

Vignette #2

Patty has recently been hired at a local community college as an administrative assistant where her job is to assist sociology department staff on a federal grant that studies cultural diversity in low-income neighborhoods. In her interview, she was asked about her word processing skills and she assured the committee that she had used many word processing applications. After her first week on the job she has been given a major assignment that involves using an unfamiliar computer application to develop a presentation to local service clubs. She has never used the application before.

Patty does not want to let her coworkers and supervisor know that she is struggling with one of her first assignments. She feels overwhelmed by the expectation to create the presentation, yet realizes that she shouldn't be expected to complete this project without training or assistance. What should Patty do?

Vignette #3

Jeremy has been searching for a job in construction for over a month. He is eighteen years old and has graduated from high school through an alternative program. During his high school years, Jeremy was arrested for possession and sale of narcotics and spent time in the county juvenile facility. Every time that he is faced with the question at the bottom of the application form that says, "Have you ever been convicted of a crime?", he knows that he jeopardizes his chances of getting hired. His mother's boyfriend has arranged for him to interview with a personal friend who is a contractor. After meeting the contractor and spending an hour touring job sites, Jeremy is told that he is hired. The contractor informs him that he will still need to fill out an application form and take a drug test before he can start work the following day. Jeremy knows his urinalysis will be fine, but he doesn't know what to think about the application. What should he do?

Vignette #4

Ellen was hired at an interstate trucking company as one of its first female mechanics. After working in the business for a month, she received an extremely positive review and was to be hired on as a permanent employee. Because the temporary employment agency that had developed the job for her did not drug test, Ellen was expected to complete a drug screening the following day.

Ellen was concerned that the marijuana that she had smoked at her graduation from mechanic school might still be detectable a month later. She talked to some of her friends and they encouraged her to go to a health food store and purchase some vitamins and minerals that might cloud the screening. She was afraid that if the vitamins and minerals didn't work, she might lose her job. Got any advice for Ellen?

LESSON 29

The Whole Is Greater Than the Sum of Its Parts

PURPOSE	**THIS LESSON IS DESIGNED TO HELP STUDENTS SOLVE PROBLEMS BY RELYING ON OTHER MEMBERS OF THE TEAM.**
	Some of the team members will be purposely "disadvantaged" to create the need for students to support one another.
LEARNING OUTCOMES	◂ Students will understand that working as a collective whole is better than working individually to accomplish the same task.
	◂ Students will value supporting the weakest member(s) of a team to improve the overall performance of the entire team.
REVIEW (5 MINUTES)	Have students discuss the amount of overlap that exists among the foundation skills (Locus of Control, Teamwork, Communication, and Problem Solving). They should be able to understand how all of the units are interrelated. Explain to students that the activity they participate in today will demonstrate how all of the foundation skills are utilized in accomplishing a goal.
REQUIRED MATERIALS	◂ White board or flip chart
	◂ Five Rectangle Template (make enough copies for each student)
	◂ Envelopes (each team should have five envelopes containing pieces from five rectangles)
	◂ Blindfold
	◂ Work Manner Of Team Members List (cut with scissors)
	◂ Work Evaluation Worksheet
LESSON 29 VOCABULARY	There is no new vocabulary for this lesson.

DESCRIPTION OF ACTIVITY:

ACTIVITY 29.1   MANY HANDS MAKE LIGHT WORK (40 MINUTES)

This activity will allow students to work as a team, communicate, problem solve, and direct their LOC internally.

◄ **Introduce** the activity by asking students if they have ever experienced situations where working together as a team accomplished more than working separately. List some examples on the board or flip chart (e.g., a carwash where each person is in charge of a portion of the vehicle vs. one where each person washes all of one vehicle; working on an assembly line where each person specializes in one task to produce more products vs. one person doing it all; in a restaurant, having specific roles for each worker vs. everyone doing everything).

◄ **Divide** the group into teams of five students. Have each team sit around a table. If you do not have multiples of five in your classroom—and thus have students left over who are not in a group—you can assign these students to the other groups as "Team Observers." Team Observers should observe the dynamics of that group and report back to the large group on what they observed.

◄ **Have each team member draw** for a specific work manner (use the Work Manner List): One team member can use his or her hands and talk but must be blindfolded; One team member can use his or her hands and talk; Two team members can use their hands but cannot talk; One team member cannot use his or her hands but can talk.

◄ **Distribute envelopes** and give the following directions:

1. Each envelope contains five pieces, some of which may be the same shape.

2. The object of the activity is for the group to make five rectangles from the contents of all envelopes.

3. The rectangles must be exactly the same.

4. The rectangles will be made from five different shapes.

5. Each team member must perform in the work manner that was drawn. If the group member acts in a manner not in accordance with the work manner he or she drew, that group must start over by putting all the pieces in the middle of the table and mixing them up.

6. You may exchange pieces only if you ask (in some manner) the person you are exchanging with for permission to exchange.

   The group will be timed by the teacher or a Team Observer. The time should be recorded on the Work Evaluation Worksheet.

◄ **Reward** the teams that finish first. Reinforce all teams for participation.

◄ **As teams complete the task** have each group complete the Work Evaluation Worksheet.

◄ **Discuss** their responses to the exercise using their Work Evaluation Worksheets.

◄ **Another version** of this activity would be to not allow anyone on either team to talk while solving the rectangle problem.

WRAP-UP/HOMEWORK

Guide the discussion in a direction that emphasizes the value of teamwork in accomplishing a goal. Attempt to encourage students to provide some more of their own examples where they worked as a member of a team to accomplish a group task that would have been more difficult to do individually. Also talk about situations where they may have needed to support other people in order to accomplish a task.

Name _____

Work Evaluation

Worksheet

Evaluate how you worked together as a team.

1. How long did it take for your team to complete the task?

2. Describe how your team accomplished the goal.

3. How did each member feel about their contribution to the team?

   ◀ Team member who was blindfolded:

   ◀ Two team members who could use their hands but couldn't talk:

   ◀ Team member who could use hands and talk:

   ◀ Team member who could not use hands but could talk:

4. Can you compare this activity with anything that has ever happened at work, at school, or at home?

Work Manner of
Team Members List

(Cut strips with scissors)

CAN USE HANDS AND TALK BUT MUST BE BLINDFOLDED
CAN USE HANDS AND TALK
CAN USE HANDS BUT NOT TALK
CAN USE HANDS BUT NOT TALK
CANNOT USE HANDS BUT CAN TALK

1. Using the two rectangles below, copy as many rectangles as there are students.
2. For each team of five students:
    a. Combine the twenty-five pieces from five rectangles.
    b. Place different combinations of pieces in each of the five envelopes (some may be the same).
    c. Make sure that no two envelopes contain the same five shapes.

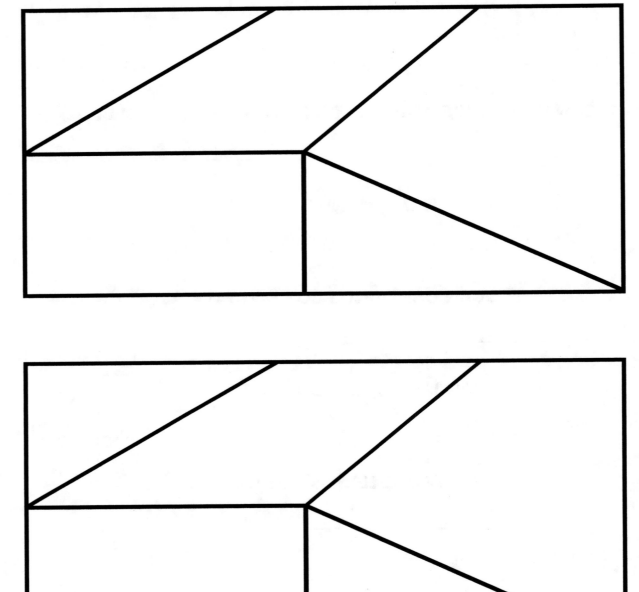

Lesson 30

Creative RADD

Purpose	**THIS LESSON WILL PROVIDE AN OPPORTUNITY FOR STUDENTS TO DO SOME CREATIVE PROBLEM SOLVING AND PERFORM IMPROMPTU SKITS DEALING WITH WORKPLACE SITUATIONS.** These skits are similar to the paper bag skits in Lesson 11. Students will use random props to create skits that apply RADD techniques to solve workplace problems involving enthusiasm, dependability, and honesty.
Learning Outcomes	◄ Students will demonstrate their ability to work as a team to create and problem solve situations that might occur on the job. ◄ Students will demonstrate their ability to use the RADD technique when problem solving those situations.
Review	Remind students about the "What's In The Bag?" skits that were created in Lesson 11. Explain that the activity will be repeated in this lesson to develop skits around enthusiasm, dependability, and honesty. Briefly review the paper bag skit guidelines from Lesson 11, and explain how the students will incorporate props to act out skits that demonstrate RADD problem solving.
Required Materials	◄ RADD Worksheet (see Lesson 25) ◄ Paper bags ◄ Five props per bag (containing items from home, school, and work that are convenient to collect—see the suggested list of props for ideas) ◄ A Suggested List of Props
Lesson 30 Vocabulary	There is no new vocabulary for this lesson.

DESCRIPTION OF ACTIVITY

ACTIVITY 30.1 RADD SKITS (40 MINUTES)

This creative activity will allow teams to demonstrate their knowledge of RADD problem solving around workplace issues involving enthusiasm, dependability, and honesty. Paper bag skits will provide an entertaining twist to the formality of RADD problem solving.

◄ **Divide** students into teams of five.

◄ **Distribute** a paper bag with props to each team.

◄ **Review** the following expectations with the group:

> Each team will be assigned a theme (enthusiasm, dependability, honesty) to create a two- to three-minute skit for the group. You can help explain the theme to each group if they do not understand the meaning or intent of the theme.

> Teams must use *all* of the props in the bag to demonstrate a RADD process of problem solving related to their assigned theme.

> Each team member must have a role in the play.

> Teams will have 15 minutes to design, rehearse, and refine their skit.

◄ **You might** want to provide some teams with space outside the classroom to rehearse their skits. If teams are outside of the classroom, it will be important to monitor them in a consistent manner.

◄ **Introduce** each skit by theme and provide positive support to teams as they present.

◄ **After** each group presents, briefly discuss the presentation with the rest of the class:

> – Did the skit utilize all the props?

> – Did the team demonstrate use of the RADD technique?

> – Did the team establish the importance of their theme in the workplace?

◄ **Repeat** the above steps for the remaining groups.

WRAP-UP/HOMEWORK

Reinforce students for their participation. Explain how RADD may provide an effective problem-solving solution to many workplace issues associated with enthusiasm, dependability, and honesty.

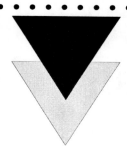

A Suggested List of Props

tie	glasses	watch	detergent
bow tie	belt	suspenders	badge
golf hat	handcuffs	rope	calculator
baseball hat	spoon	harmonica	novel/book
pen	phone	beeper	ball
pop bottle	keyboard	alarm clock	marker
food container	dictionary	whistle	flashlight
clothes hanger	banana	headband	bat
leash	lab coat	hard hat	portable radio
videotape	notebook	ruler	date book
candle	mouse pad	extension cord	screwdriver
key	stapler	paper clip	scotch tape

LESSON 31

Making More *W.A.G.E.S.* Again

PURPOSE	**THIS LESSON PROVIDES A REVIEW OF THE ENTIRE COURSE.** The students will go over the foundation skills and attitudes associated with being a successful worker that were introduced in Lesson 2 and that have been the basis of the entire curriculum. They again will play the "Making *W.A.G.E.S.*" game to review and demonstrate their knowledge of Locus of Control, Teamwork, Communication, and Problem Solving.
LEARNING OUTCOMES	◄ Students will demonstrate mastery knowledge of the four foundation skills (Locus of Control, Teamwork, Communication, and Problem Solving) necessary to make successful connections on the job. ◄ Students will demonstrate mastery knowledge of the attitudes (dependability, honesty, and enthusiasm) associated with effective social skills on the job.
REVIEW (5 MINUTES)	Review the rules for playing the final round of the "Making *W.A.G.E.S.* Contest." Explain to students that this will be their last opportunity to play the game and demonstrate their knowledge of the vocabulary and concepts associated with the curriculum.
REQUIRED MATERIALS	◄ "Making *W.A.G.E.S.*" game cards (see Appendix) ◄ "Making *W.A.G.E.S.*" Tally Sheet (see Lesson 2) ◄ Small treats or other incentives
LESSON 31 VOCABULARY	There is no new vocabulary for this lesson.

DESCRIPTION OF ACTIVITY

ACTIVITY 31.1   REVISITING THE "MAKING *W.A.G.E.S.*" GAME (35 MINUTES)

Playing the game will allow students to compete for incentives by demonstrating their level of knowledge of the course content. This is the final time the game will be played. During this activity, students should be able to demonstrate a higher level of learning and performance than the other times they played the game.

- ◀ **Divide** students into teams (with a maximum of three teams). Provide each team with a "Making *W.A.G.E.S.*" Tally Sheet.

- ◀ **Explain** to students that they will be asked to define or perform certain tasks contained on the back of cards in each of the four content areas; tasks are worth 100 to 500 points. Tell them that "the higher the number of points, the more difficult the problem." As teams choose cards and correctly answer the problems presented on the back of each card, members will keep track of points scored with each round played. It's a good idea for you to keep track of the points on the board or overhead, as well. In addition, you will need to judge students' performance on some of the questions to determine if they earned the points.

- ◀ **Requirements:** Each team will get one chance to solve each problem and earn points. Each team will be expected to select problems with varying point values for at least three rounds. They must choose problems with values that cannot be repeated until they have played three rounds (i.e., 100, 300, 200, then 100 is okay ; 100, 200, 100 is not okay).

- ◀ **The object** of the game is to score the highest number of points in the amount of time available. At the end of play, total points earned throughout the game determines the winner. Incentives for the winners should be given (e.g., free time, treats, etc.).

WRAP-UP/HOMEWORK

Reward students with incentives and celebrate the final round of the "Making *W.A.G.E.S.*" game. Remind them that only two lessons remain. Explain that each of these lessons will involve final assessments of their knowledge and skill in problem solving.

LESSON 32

Let's RADD Our Problems
(Part One)

PURPOSE	**THIS LESSON ALLOWS STUDENTS TO DEMONSTRATE THEIR KNOWLEDGE OF THE RADD PROBLEM-SOLVING PROCESS.** Students work in teams to problem solve the eight vignettes from Lessons 27 and 28, and to present the problem in a role-play. They then participate in a team discussing each step of the RADD process.
LEARNING OUTCOMES	◄ Students will demonstrate their ability to work as a team to problem solve situations that might occur on the job. ◄ Students will demonstrate their ability to use the RADD technique when problem solving those situations.
REVIEW	Ask students to get out their completed RADD Worksheets from Lessons 27 and 28—the dependability and honesty lessons. Tell them that they will be working in teams during this lesson and the next lesson to demonstrate their ability to use the RADD technique on the eight dependability and honesty vignettes.
REQUIRED MATERIALS	◄ Flip chart or white board/chalkboard ◄ Are You Dependable? Vignettes (see Lesson 27) ◄ Honesty Vignettes (see Lesson 28) ◄ RADD Worksheet (see Lesson 25) ◄ CBM Vocabulary Test #6
LESSON 32 VOCABULARY	There is no new vocabulary for this lesson.

DESCRIPTION OF ACTIVITY

ACTIVITY 32.1   RADD DEMONSTRATIONS (45 MINUTES)

This activity will allow students to demonstration their application of the RADD technique on the eight vignettes from Lessons 27 and 28.

◀ Divide students into teams of three and assign each group a vignette. Another option is to have each group choose the vignette they would like to RADD. Do your best to accommodate their choices.

◀ Once the teams and vignettes are assigned, hand out a RADD Worksheet to each team and give them 20 minutes to decide how they want to RADD their vignette. The team members should use the RADD worksheets they completed as homework for Lessons 27 and 28 to compare each other's ideas on how to RADD the problem. They then must role-play their version of solving the problem to come to a group decision on what to present to the rest of the class.

◀ After role-playing the vignette, each team member must comment on some portion of the RADD technique that was used to solve the problem (i.e., Recognize, Alternatives, Decide, and Determine). For example, one person can present the first step of recognizing the problem, one person can present the alternatives, and one person can present the group's final decision and why it was chosen.

CBM (10 MINUTES)

Hand out the CBM Vocabulary Test #6 to the students. Time them for seven minutes, then collect their tests. Record the results and compare them to previous CBM tests.

WRAP-UP/HOMEWORK

Tell students that the remaining teams will present during the next lesson. Praise students for their participation. Inform students that the Problem-Solving Post-Test will be administered at the conclusion of the unit. They should be encouraged to participate fully in the remaining activities so that they will score well on the scenario that is presented in the post-test.

LESSON 33

Let's RADD Our Problems
(Part Two)

PURPOSE	**THIS LESSON IS A CONTINUATION OF LESSON 32 AND ALLOWS STUDENTS TO DEMONSTRATE THEIR KNOWLEDGE OF THE RADD PROBLEM-SOLVING PROCESS.** Students work in teams to problem solve the eight vignettes from Lessons 27 and 28, and present the problem in a role-play. They then participate in a team discussing each step of the RADD process.
LEARNING OUTCOMES	◀ Students will demonstrate their ability to work as a team to problem solve situations that might occur on the job. ◀ Students will demonstrate their ability to use the RADD technique when problem solving those situations.
PROBLEM-SOLVING POST-TEST (10 MINUTES)	Hand out the Problem-Solving Post-Test, and ask students to complete the questions as you read the test out loud. Make sure that every student marks an answer to each question in the appropriate space. Briefly review the "best" answers with the students.
REVIEW	Tell students this lesson will be a continuation of the last lesson. Those teams that did not present during Lesson 27 will present today. Have students get out their dependability and honesty vignettes so that they can refer to them as each group presents.
REQUIRED MATERIALS	◀ Are You Dependable? Vignettes (see Lesson 27) ◀ Honesty Vignettes (see Lesson 28) ◀ RADD Worksheet (see Lesson 25) ◀ Flip chart or white board/chalkboard ◀ Unit Five Mastery Vocabulary Test ◀ Problem-Solving Post-Test
LESSON 33 VOCABULARY	There is no new vocabulary for this lesson.

DESCRIPTION OF ACTIVITY

ACTIVITY 33.1   RADD DEMONSTRATIONS (45 MINUTES)

This activity will allow students to demonstrate their application of the RADD technique on the eight vignettes from Lessons 27 and 28.

‹ Divide students into teams of three and assign each group a vignette. Another option is to have each group choose the vignette they would like to RADD. Do your best to accommodate their choices.

‹ Once the teams and vignettes are assigned, hand out a RADD Worksheet to each team and give them 20 minutes to decide how they want to RADD their vignette. The team members should use the RADD Worksheets they completed as homework for Lessons 27 and 28 to compare each other's ideas on how to RADD the problem. They then must role-play their version of solving the problem to come to a group decision on what to present to the rest of the class.

‹ After role-playing the vignette, each team member must comment on some portion of the RADD technique that was used to solve the problem (i.e., Recognize, Alternatives, Decide and Determine). For example, one person can present the first step of recognizing the problem, one person can present the alternatives, and one person can present the group's final decision and why it was chosen.

MASTERY TEST (5 MINUTES)

Give students the Unit Five Mastery Vocabulary Test (see Appendix), and time them for five minutes. Record results and compare to earlier tests.

WRAP-UP/HOMEWORK

Reinforce students for their participation in the lesson. Tell them that this concludes the W.A.G.E.S. curriculum. Use the remaining time to discuss possible improvements that might be made to strengthen the lessons and content.

Problem-Solving
Post-Test

Mike has a new job on an assembly line in a factory. He wants to make a good impression on his boss and is working hard to figure out just what he has to do in order to perform the job well.

However, he is having trouble working as quickly as he needs to and the work materials are beginning to spill off the assembly line and onto the floor.

He tries even harder but gets farther behind. As he tries to work faster, he starts to think his coworkers are not doing their jobs, which is the major cause of his problem, and realizes that they are not offering to help him out. His boss comes up just then and sees the mess and does not appear happy.

Questions
(Read out loud to the students; be sure that every student marks an answer for each question on an answer sheet)

Please rate each of the following statements on the following scale:

3 - The statement is exactly in line with your impression from the scenario that was just read.
2 - The statement is somewhat in line with your impression from the scenario that was just read.
1 - The statement is not at all in line with your impression from the scenario that was just read.

So, if the statement I read is exactly consistent with what you believe to be true from this scenario, mark your answer with a 3. If the statement I read is somewhat consistent with what you believe to be true from this scenario, mark your answer with a 2. If the statement I read is not at all consistent with what you believe to be true from this scenario, mark your answer with a 1.

RECOGNIZE

1. ____Mike wants to do well on his new job.

2. ____Mike is working hard but probably doesn't completely know how to do his job.

3. ____Mike isn't working hard at all.

4. ____The primary thing that Mike wants to do is just get through the day, no matter how well he works.

5. ____The problems Mike is having are all due to his coworkers.

6. ____The boss is totally wrong if he gets mad at Mike.

7. ____The boss should first be angry with the coworkers and should not be concerned with Mike's work problem.

8. ____The boss should be irritated about Mike's low level of production because he has the responsibility for production and the smooth operation of the business.

9. ____Mike's coworkers obviously are testing him because he is a new employee and because he is a "kid."

10. ____Mike's coworkers are not aware that he is having a problem.

Ok, now I am going provide some alternatives that Mike could do on the job in response to this problem. I want you to rate each of these statements on the following scale:

3 -The alternative is very effective in addressing the problem.
2 -The alternative is somewhat effective in addressing the problem.
1 -The alternative is not at all effective in addressing the problem.

So, if you think an alternative will be effective in addressing the problem, mark your answer with a 3. If you think the alternative would be somewhat effective in addressing the problem, mark your answer with a 2. If you think the alternative will be ineffective in addressing the problem, mark your answer with a 1.

ALTERNATIVES

11. ____Mike should tell his boss that the problem is the fault of his coworkers.

12. ____Mike should yell at his boss; it is unfair to have a new person do all this work.

13. ____Mike should just try to work harder and ignore the coworkers.

14. ____Mike should level with the boss, telling him about the problem and ask for advice.

15. ____Mike should wait until the boss leaves and then go over and yell at the coworkers.

16. ____Mike should go to his coworkers and politely ask for some help.

17. ____Mike should quit the job.

In this section I want you to determine the effectiveness of choosing each of the following alternatives as a plan of action. So, if you think an alternative will be effective as a plan of action, mark your answer with a 3. If you think the alternative would be somewhat effective in addressing the problem, mark your answer with a 2. If you think the alternative will be ineffective in addressing the problem, mark your answer with a 1.

DECIDE AND DETERMINE

18. ____Quit the job.

19. ____Wait until the boss leaves and then talk to the coworkers.

20. ____Tell the boss that the problem is the fault of all the coworkers.

21. ____Level with the boss, tell him about the problem, and ask for advice.

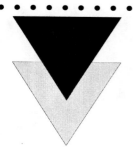

Agreed-Upon Ratings for Problem Solving Vignette

Post Test (Mike)

Lesson	1	2	3	4	5	6	7	8	9	10	11	12	13	14	15	16	17	18	19	20
Answer	3	3	1	1	1	1	1	3	1	2	1	1	1	3	1	3	1	1	2	1

Appendix

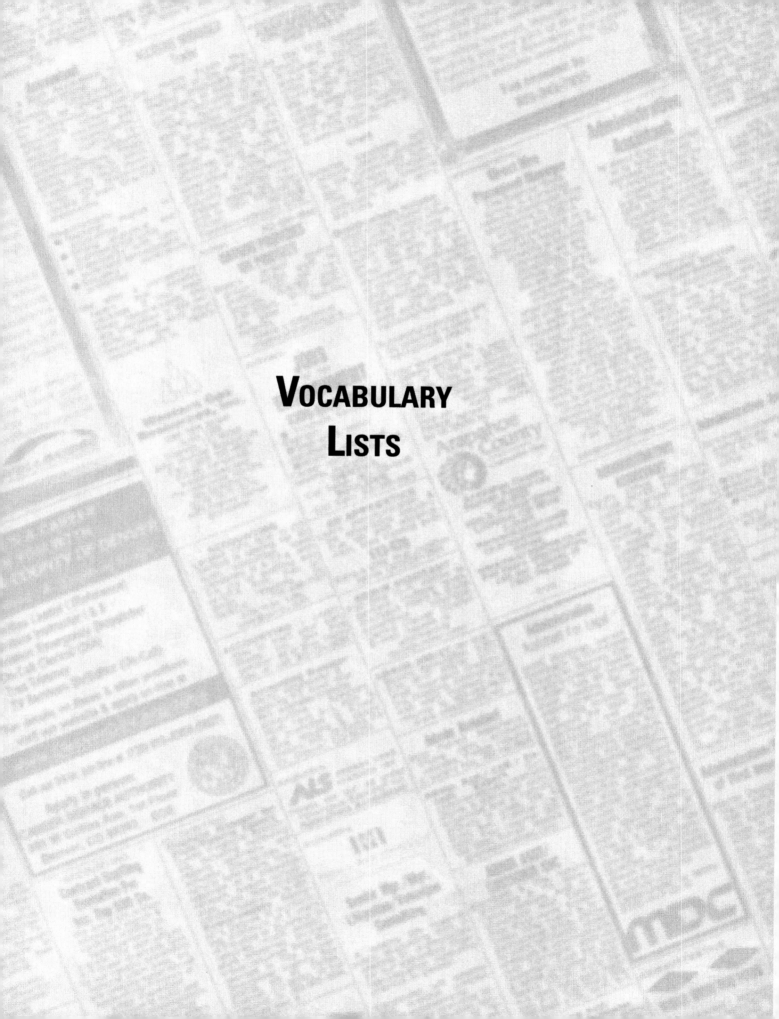

VOCABULARY
LISTS

Unit One

Vocabulary List

Workplace Social Skills: Those social interaction skills that are necessary for a person to succeed in gaining and maintaining employment.

Foundation Skills: Those social skills or attitudes that are most important for experiencing success on the job. Foundation skills include:

Locus of Control (LOC): The "location" of an individual's sense of personal control or responsibility over actions and events. Example: people who tend to blame others have a locus of control that is located outside of themselves.

Teamwork: The measure of a person's ability to work with others to accomplish a task. Example: a group of workers efficiently moving furniture into a home.

Communication: The measure of how well a person makes his or her thoughts and feelings known to others. Example: maintaining good eye contact with your employer while discussing work tasks.

Problem Solving: The measure of how well a person can develop strategies for overcoming obstacles or issues with people or situations. Example: figuring out how to ask your boss for more hours on the job.

Attitudes: Those qualities that a person needs to reflect a positive attitude on the job. They include:

Dependability: The measure of how much a person can be relied upon by coworkers and supervisors to perform work-related tasks. Example: showing up on time ready to work every day.

Honesty: The measure of how much a person is truthful to and respectful of co-workers and supervisors. Example: confessing about losing a tool that was important to all workers in the shop.

Enthusiasm: The measure of how much a person enjoys his or her work, and expresses that enjoyment appropriately to others. Example: encouraging coworkers to eat lunch together once a week.

Unit Two

Vocabulary List

LESSON 3

Internal Locus of Control: "Internal locus of control" is a measure that determines how much self-control and responsibility a person has for his or her own behavior. People with a strong internal locus of control tend to "own," or take credit or blame for, their actions. Example: apologizing for being late to a meeting without making excuses.

External Locus of Control: "External locus of control" is a measure of how little self-control and responsibility a person has for his or her own behavior. People with a strong external locus of control tend to "moan" about, or place credit or blame for, their actions. Example: whining or making excuses about being late.

LESSON 4

Role-Play: To act out a situation, behavior, or attitude as if it were really happening. Example: "becoming" or acting like an angry student who makes excuses about not doing his or her homework.

LESSON 6

Firecracker: A word, statement, or action that makes a person "go off" and begin to lose self-control. Example: being called "stupid" by a coworker when you ask an honest question.

Pressure Gauge: The physical/emotional indicator that signifies someone is under stress and losing control. For example, sweaty palms, clenched fists, a red face, a tight stomach, elevated breathing, and a suffocating feeling are all indicators of starting to lose self-control.

LESSON 7

Cooling Off: What someone does to get things back under control. Example: counting to ten before responding to an insult.

Affirmation: A personal statement or thought about oneself that is positive and hopeful. Example: having a thought like, "I am liked by my fellow employees," after your boss criticizes your work.

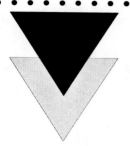

Unit Three

Vocabulary List

LESSON 10

Self-Advocacy: A person's ability to speak up, defend, or promote his or her opinion or belief. Example: being able to let a coworker know they are letting down the team by being late to work.

Consensus: When every member of a group is willing to go along with the general feeling of the group. For example, Ted may not particularly agree with his two friends, but they were so excited that he went along with their desires.

LESSON 11

Prop: An article used in a skit/play to make the setting or action seem more realistic. Examples: an eye patch worn to define the role of a pirate, or a tie-dyed shirt to define the role of a 60's hippie.

Unit Four

Vocabulary List

Lesson 14

One-Way Communication: When one person is doing all of the talking and no one else asks questions or interacts with the person.

Two-Way Communication: When people interact, listen, and ask questions of one another to clearly understand what is said.

Nonverbal Communication: What an individual says with his or her body, facial expressions, tone of voice and posture. Slumped shoulders, no eye contact, crossed arms, a low voice, and fidgeting are examples of nonverbal communication that should be avoided during an interview. Eye contact, smiling, a clear voice, and good posture are examples of nonverbal communication that should be utilized during an interview.

Lesson 16

Paraphrase: A communication style where you state in your own words what you thought someone just said. Examples: "Do you mean the primer needs to dry for two hours before I begin finishing the trim?" or "Are you telling me that I should have waited to begin mopping the floor?"

Lesson 17

Accepting Criticism: When a person is able to respond with a positive attitude to a supervisor, coworker, or customer who wants something done differently. Example: being able to smile while your editor tells you that a chapter needs to be rewritten for the twelfth time.

Feedback: Information that is provided as a response to an action, event, or behavior that can be used to create improvement or change. Example: "Mike's boss provided him with feedback that allowed him to become the company's leading salesman."

Internal Response: A response that reflects an internal locus of control (i.e. owning, responsibility, self-control). For example, an internal response to a demanding customer might be: "I'm sorry you feel so badly about the delay, can I offer you something to drink?"

External Response: A response that reflects an external locus of control (i.e. moaning, blaming, whining). For example, an external response to a demanding customer might be: "I can't help it if we are shorthanded!"

Lesson 18

Passive Communication Style: When a person gives the impression that everything is okay, even when it is not. Examples: not communicating directly with a coworker, avoiding eye contact, withholding feelings, and maintaining silence.

Aggressive Communication Style: When a person states how he or she feels and thinks without considering the feelings of others. Examples: communicating with put-downs, sarcasm, and an air of superiority around coworkers.

Assertive Communication Style: When a person can communicate with confidence and sensitivity. Example: being able to refuse a request from a coworker without making them mad.

"I" messages: Statements containing "I" that are used to express opinions, thoughts, or feelings. These messages tend to represent statements of ownership from people who are acting with an internal locus of control. Example: "I have a hard time waiting in long lines and being around lots of people."

"You" messages: Statements containing "You" that are used to express opinions, thoughts, or feelings. These messages tend to represent statements of whining and blaming by people projecting an external locus of control. Example: "You shop entirely too much."

LESSON 19

Vent: To get things "off one's chest". An expression of anger and frustration over a situation or behavior. For example, "Mr. Hicks, you make me sick the way you treat all of us during the holidays!"

Empathy: To be able to see things from the other person's perspective. For example, "Mr. Hicks, I understand why the holidays are a tough time of year for you."

LESSON 20

Enthusiasm: The measure of how much a person enjoys his or her work, and expresses that enjoyment appropriately to others. Example: encouraging coworkers to eat lunch together once a week.

Optimism: An attitude that allows one to see the bright side in situations. Example: the ability to accept being laid off from a job because it provides a good opportunity to find a better one.

Lesson 21

Interviewer: The person who conducts the job interview. For example, the manager of a restaurant might interview potential employees.

Interviewee: The person who seeks the job and must answer questions in order to be evaluated by the interviewer. For example, a 17-year-old high school senior interviews for a job at a fast food restaurant.

Greeting: The way an interviewee introduces himself or herself to an interviewer. For example, a firm handshake, eye contact, a smile, "Nice to meet you, _____ ," good posture, and telling the interviewer your name are aspects of a strong greeting.

Unit Five

Vocabulary List

LESSON 25

Problem: Any time a difficult situation occurs where there is no clear solution. For example, a flat tire happens on the way to work.

Outcome: What needs to be accomplished by solving the problem. For example, what is the most important thing that needs to happen now that the tire is flat?

Alternatives: Potential solutions to solving the problem. Examples: call work; start walking; call emergency road service; change the tire.

Dependability: The measure of how much a person can be relied upon by coworkers and supervisors to perform work-related tasks.

LESSON 27

Responsibility: A sense or feeling of ownership that leads one to act in a dependable manner. Example: the feeling one might have when one is in charge of opening and closing at a restaurant.

Punctuality: Another way of saying "on time." Punctuality means showing up to work, meetings, and events before they begin.

Lesson 28

Honesty: A personal quality that a person possesses that creates a strong sense of faith and trust in their character. For example, people who possess honesty are not accused of stealing when cash disappears from the register.

Exaggeration: Stretching the truth to make a favorable impression. For example, someone might stretch the truth by telling the supervisor he or she isn't feeling well so he or she can go home early. The person may only have a headache but really want to get home to deal with a needy family member.

CBM
Vocabulary
Tests

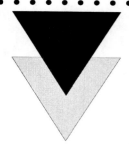

Name _____

CBM Vocabulary Test #1

DEFINITION	WRITE THE WORD
A measure of how little self-control and responsibility a person has for his or her own behavior; people that tend to moan about, or place credit or blame for, their actions have it.	
To act out a situation, behavior, or attitude as if it were really happening.	
What someone does to get things back under control.	
A person's ability to speak up, defend, or promote his or her opinion or belief.	
An article used in a skit/play to make the setting or action seem more realistic.	
What a person says with his or her body, facial expressions, tone of voice, and posture.	
Statements that are used to express opinions, thoughts, or feelings and that tend to represent statements of ownership.	
The measure of how much a person enjoys his or her work and expresses that enjoyment appropriately to others.	
The way an interviewee introduces himself or herself to an interviewer.	
Anytime a difficult situation occurs where there is no clear solution.	
What needs to be accomplished by solving the problem.	
A sense or feeling of ownership that leads one to act in a dependable manner.	
Another way of saying "on time." For example, showing up to work, meetings, and events before they begin.	
A personal quality a person possesses that creates a strong sense of faith and trust in their character.	
Stretching the truth to make a favorable impression.	

CBM Vocabulary Test #1

Answer Sheet

DEFINITION	WORD
A measure of how little self-control and responsibility a person has for his or her own behavior; people that tend to moan about, or place credit or blame for, their actions have it.	**External Locus of Control**
To act out a situation, behavior, or attitude as if it were really happening.	**Role-Play**
What someone does to get things back under control.	**Cooling Off**
A person's ability to speak up, defend, or promote his or her opinion or belief.	**Self-Advocacy**
An article used in a skit/play to make the setting or action seem more realistic.	**Prop**
What a person says with his or her body, facial expressions, tone of voice, and posture.	**Nonverbal Communication**
Statements that are used to express opinions, thoughts, or feelings and that tend to represent statements of ownership from people who are acting with an internal locus of control.	**"I" Messages**
The measure of how much a person enjoys his or her work and expresses that enjoyment appropriately to others.	**Enthusiasm**
The way an interviewee introduces himself or herself to an interviewer.	**Greeting**
Anytime a difficult situation occurs where there is no clear solution.	**Problem**
What needs to be accomplished by solving the problem.	**Outcome**
A sense or feeling of ownership that leads one to act in a dependable manner.	**Responsibility**
Another way of saying "on time." For example, showing up to work, meetings, and events before they begin.	**Punctuality**
A personal quality a person possesses that creates a strong sense of faith and trust in their character.	**Honesty**
Stretching the truth to make a favorable impression.	**Exaggeration**

Name _____

CBM Vocabulary Test #2

DEFINITION	WRITE THE WORD
A word, statement, or action that makes a person "go off" and begin to lose self-control.	
A personal statement or thought about oneself that is positive and hopeful.	
A person's ability to speak up, defend, or promote his or her opinion or belief.	
An article used in a skit/play to make the setting or action seem more realistic.	
A response that reflects an internal locus of control (i.e., owning, responsibility, self-control).	
A response that reflects an external locus of control (i.e., moaning, blaming, whining).	
When a person gives the impression that everything is okay, even when it is not.	
Statements that tend to express opinions, thoughts, or feelings through whining and blaming others.	
To get things "off one's chest." An expression of anger and frustration over a situation or behavior.	
To be able to see things from the other person's perspective.	
The measure of how much a person enjoys his or her work and expresses that enjoyment appropriately to others.	
An attitude that allows one to see the bright side in situations.	
Any time a difficult situation occurs where there is no clear solution.	
A sense or feeling of ownership that leads one to act in a dependable manner.	
A personal quality a person possesses that creates a strong sense of faith and trust in his or her character.	

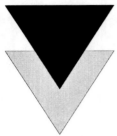

CBM Vocabulary Test #2

Answer Sheet

DEFINITION	WORD
A word, statement, or action that makes a person "go off" and begin to lose self-control.	Firecracker
A personal statement or thought about oneself that is positive and hopeful.	Affirmation
A person's ability to speak up, defend, or promote his or her opinion or belief.	Self-Advocacy
An article used in a skit/play to make the setting or action seem more realistic.	Prop
A response that reflects an internal locus of control (i.e., owning, responsibility, self-control).	Internal Response
A response that reflects an external locus of control (i.e., moaning, blaming, whining).	External Response
When a person gives the impression that everything is okay, even when it is not.	Passive Communication Style
Statements that tend to express opinions, thoughts, or feelings through whining and blaming others.	"You" Messages
To get things "off one's chest." An expression of anger and frustration over a situation or behavior.	Vent
To be able to see things from the other person's perspective.	Empathy
The measure of how much a person enjoys his or her work and expresses that enjoyment appropriately to others.	Enthusiasm
An attitude that allows one to see the bright side in situations.	Optimism
Any time a difficult situation occurs where there is no clear solution.	Problem
A sense or feeling of ownership that leads one to act in a dependable manner.	Responsibility
A personal quality that a person possesses that creates a strong sense of faith and trust in his or her character.	Honesty

CBM Vocabulary Test #3

DEFINITION	WRITE THE WORD
The location of an individual's sense of personal control or responsibility over actions and events.	
A measure that determines how much self-control and responsibility a person has for his or her own behavior; people that tend to own, or take credit or blame for, their actions have this.	
To act out a situation, behavior, or attitude as if it were really happening.	
The physical/emotional indicators that signify someone is under stress and losing control: sweaty palms, clenched fists, red face, tight stomach, elevated breathing.	
What someone does to get things back under control.	
When every member of a group is willing to go along with the general feeling of the group.	
When one person is doing all of the talking and others don't ask questions or interact with the person.	
When people interact, listen, and ask questions of one another to clearly understand what is said.	
A communication style where you state in your own words what you think someone just said.	
When a person states how they feel and think without considering the feelings of others.	
When a person can communicate with assured strength and sensitivity.	
The person who conducts the job interview.	
What needs to be accomplished by solving the problem.	
Potential solutions to solving the problem.	
A sense or feeling of ownership that leads one to act in a dependable manner.	

CBM Vocabulary Test #3
Answer Sheet

DEFINITION	WORD
The location of an individual's sense of personal control or responsibility over actions and events.	**Locus of Control**
A measure that determines how much self-control and responsibility a person has for his or her own behavior; people that tend to own, or take credit or blame for, their actions have this.	**Internal Locus of Control**
To act out a situation, behavior, or attitude as if it were really happening.	**Role-Play**
The physical/emotional indicators that signify someone is under stress and losing control: sweaty palms, clenched fists, red face, tight stomach, elevated breathing.	**Pressure Gauge**
What someone does to get things back under control.	**Cooling Off**
When every member of a group is willing to go along with the general feeling of the group.	**Consensus**
When one person is doing all of the talking and others don't ask questions or interact with the person.	**One-Way Communication**
When people interact, listen, and ask questions of one another to clearly understand what is said.	**Two-Way Communication**
A communication style where you state in your own words what you think someone just said.	**Paraphrase**
When a person states how they feel and think without considering the feelings of others.	**Aggressive Communication Style**
When a person can communicate with assured strength and sensitivity.	**Assertive Communication Style**
The person who conducts the job interview.	**Interviewer**
What needs to be accomplished by solving the problem.	**Outcome**
Potential solutions to solving the problem.	**Alternatives**
A sense or feeling of ownership that leads one to act in a dependable manner.	**Responsibility**

Name _____

CBM Vocabulary Test #4

DEFINITION	WRITE THE WORD
A measure of how little self-control and responsibility a person has for his or her own behavior; people that tend to moan about, or place credit or blame for, their actions have this.	
To act out a situation, behavior, or attitude as if it were really happening.	
What someone does to get things back under control.	
A person's ability to speak up, defend, or promote their opinion or belief.	
When one person is doing all of the talking and others don't ask questions or interact with the person.	
When people interact, listen, and ask questions of one another to clearly understand what is said.	
When a person gives the impression that everything is okay, even when it is not.	
When a person can communicate with assured strength and sensitivity.	
To be able to see things from the other person's perspective.	
An attitude that allows one to see the bright side in situations.	
The person who seeks the job and must answer questions in order to be evaluated by the interviewer.	
The way an interviewee introduces himself or herself to an interviewer.	
Any time a difficult situation occurs where there is no clear solution.	
The measure of how much a person can be relied upon by coworkers and supervisors to perform work-related tasks.	
A personal quality that a person possesses that creates a strong sense of faith and trust in their character.	

CBM Vocabulary Test #4

Answer Sheet

DEFINITION	WORD
A measure of how little self-control and responsibility a person has for his or her own behavior; people that tend to moan about, or place credit or blame for, their actions have this.	**External Locus of Control**
To act out a situation, behavior, or attitude as if it were really happening.	**Role-Play**
What someone does to get things back under control.	**Cooling Off**
A person's ability to speak up, defend, or promote their opinion or belief.	**Self-Advocacy**
When one person is doing all of the talking and others don't ask questions or interact with the person.	**One-Way Communication**
When people interact, listen, and ask questions of one another to clearly understand what is said.	**Two-Way Communication**
When a person gives the impression that everything is okay, even when it is not.	**Passive Communication Style**
When a person can communicate with assured strength and sensitivity.	**Assertive Communication Style**
To be able to see things from the other person's perspective.	**Empathy**
An attitude that allows one to see the bright side in situations.	**Optimism**
The person who seeks the job and must answer questions in order to be evaluated by the interviewer.	**Interviewee**
The way an interviewee introduces himself or herself to an interviewer.	**Greeting**
Any time a difficult situation occurs where there is no clear solution.	**Problem**
The measure of how much a person can be relied upon by coworkers and supervisors to perform work-related tasks.	**Dependability**
A personal quality that a person possesses that creates a strong sense of faith and trust in their character.	**Honesty**

Name _____

CBM Vocabulary Test #5

DEFINITION   **WRITE THE WORD**

A communication style where you state in your own words what you think someone just said.

A measure that determines how much self-control and responsibility a person has for his or her own behavior; people that tend to own, or take credit or blame for, their actions have this.

A personal quality a person possesses that creates a strong sense of faith and trust in their character.

A response that reflects an external locus of control (i.e., moaning, blaming, whining).

A word, statement, or action that makes a person go off and begin to lose self-control.

An article used in a skit/play to make the setting or action seem more realistic.

Positive feedback that is aimed at improving performance or a situation as opposed to being negative and destructive.

Statements containing the word "You" that are used to express opinions, thoughts, or feelings and that tend to represent statements of whining and blaming.

Stretching the truth to make a favorable impression.

To admit a mistake or accept responsibility for an error.

The measure of how much a person enjoys his or her work and expresses that enjoyment appropriately to others.

To get things "off one's chest." An expression of anger and frustration over a situation or behavior.

What needs to be accomplished by solving the problem.

When a person can communicate with assured strength and sensitivity.

When a person gives the impression that everything is okay, even when it is not.

CBM Vocabulary Test #5

Answer Sheet

DEFINITION	WORD
A communication style where you state in your own words what you think someone just said.	**Paraphrase**
A measure that determines how much self-control and responsibility a person has for his or her own behavior; people that tend to own, or take credit or blame for, their actions have this.	**Internal Locus of Control**
A personal quality a person possesses that creates a strong sense of faith and trust in their character.	**Honesty**
A response that reflects an external locus of control (i.e., moaning, blaming, whining).	**External Response**
A word, statement, or action that makes a person go off and begin to lose self-control.	**Firecracker**
An article used in a skit/play to make the setting or action seem more realistic.	**Prop**
Positive feedback that is aimed at improving performance or a situation as opposed to being negative and destructive.	**Constructive Criticism**
Statements containing the word "You" that are used to express opinions, thoughts, or feelings and that tend to represent statements of whining and blaming.	**"You" Messages**
Stretching the truth to make a favorable impression.	**Exaggeration**
To admit a mistake or accept responsibility for an error.	**Confess**
The measure of how much a person enjoys his or her work and expresses that enjoyment appropriately to others.	**Enthusiasm**
To get things "off one's chest." An expression of anger and frustration over a situation or behavior.	**Vent**
What needs to be accomplished by solving the problem.	**Outcome**
When a person can communicate with assured strength and sensitivity.	**Assertive Communication Style**
When a person gives the impression that everything is okay, even when it is not.	**Passive Communication Style**

Name _____

CBM Vocabulary Test #6

DEFINITION	WRITE THE WORD
The location of an individual's sense of personal control or responsibility over actions and events.	
A word, statement, or action that makes a person "go off" and begin to lose self-control.	
The physical/emotional indicators that signify someone is under stress and losing control: sweaty palms, clenched fists, red face, tight stomach, elevated breathing.	
A personal statement or thought about oneself that is positive and hopeful.	
When every member of a group is willing to go along with the general feeling of the group.	
When one person is doing all of the talking and others don't ask questions or interact with the person.	
A communication style where you state in your own words what you think someone just said.	
Information that is provided as a response to an action, event, or behavior that can be used to create improvement or change.	
A response that reflects an internal locus of control (i.e., owning, responsibility, self-control).	
A response that reflects an external locus of control (i.e., moaning, blaming, whining).	
To be able to see things from the other person's perspective.	
The person who conducts the job interview.	
The way an interviewee introduces himself or herself to an interviewer.	
What an individual says with his or her body, facial expressions, tone of voice, and posture.	
Another way of saying "on time." For example, showing up to work, meetings, and events before they begin.	

CBM Vocabulary Test #6

Answer Sheet

DEFINITION	WORD
The location of an individual's sense of personal control or responsibility over actions and events.	**Locus of Control**
A word, statement, or action that makes a person "go off" and begin to lose self-control.	**Firecracker**
The physical/emotional indicators that signify someone is under stress and losing control: sweaty palms, clenched fists, red face, tight stomach, elevated breathing.	**Pressure Gauge**
A personal statement or thought about oneself that is positive and hopeful.	**Affirmation**
When every member of a group is willing to go along with the general feeling of the group.	**Consensus**
When one person is doing all of the talking and others don't ask questions or interact with the person.	**One-Way Communication**
A communication style where you state in your own words what you think someone just said.	**Paraphrase**
Information that is provided as a response to an action, event, or behavior that can be used to create improvement or change.	**Feedback**
A response that reflects an internal locus of control (i.e., owning, responsibility, self-control).	**Internal Response**
A response that reflects an external locus of control (i.e., moaning, blaming, whining).	**External Response**
To be able to see things from the other person's perspective.	**Empathy**
The person who conducts the job interview.	**Interviewer**
The way an interviewee introduces himself or herself to an interviewer.	**Greeting**
What an individual says with his or her body, facial expressions, tone of voice, and posture.	**Nonverbal Communication**
Another way of saying "on time." For example, showing up to work, meetings, and events before they begin.	**Punctuality**

Making
W.A.G.E.S.
Game Cards

Q "Moaning" demonstrates an _____ locus of control.

100 POINTS
LOCUS OF CONTROL

Q Blaming your boss for talking too quickly demonstrates an _____ LOC.

200 POINTS
LOCUS OF CONTROL

Q "Owning" demonstrates an _____ locus of control.

100 POINTS
LOCUS OF CONTROL

Q Apologizing to your coworker demonstrates an _____ LOC.

200 POINTS
LOCUS OF CONTROL

Q Define locus of control.

100 POINTS
LOCUS OF CONTROL

Q You arrive to work late and tell your boss your alarm did not go off. What kind of LOC is this?

200 POINTS
LOCUS OF CONTROL

Q Internal locus of control involves placing blame or credit on _____.

100 POINTS
LOCUS OF CONTROL

Q Telling your coworker you are angry at the boss for making you redo your work is an _____ LOC.

200 POINTS
LOCUS OF CONTROL

Q External locus of control involves placing blame or credit on _____.

100 POINTS
LOCUS OF CONTROL

Q "Sorry that I am late" suggests what about a person's LOC?

200 POINTS
LOCUS OF CONTROL

A External.

A External.

A Internal.

A Internal.

A External.

A The location of an individual's sense of personal control or responsibility over actions and events.

A External.

A Yourself.

A It is internal/owning.

A Someone or something other than yourself.

Q Make a similar statement that is the opposite of the LOC used in this statement: "We increased production because the boss was looking over our shoulders."

300 POINTS
LOCUS OF CONTROL

 Q "Some people have all the luck" suggests an _____ LOC. Why?

400 POINTS
LOCUS OF CONTROL

 Q Define "firecracker" as used when referring to a person's self-control.

300 POINTS
LOCUS OF CONTROL

 Q "My boss hates me!" suggests a person has what type of LOC? Why?

400 POINTS
LOCUS OF CONTROL

 Q You tell the boss you have been working hard to improve the quality of the product. Is this internal or external LOC?

300 POINTS
LOCUS OF CONTROL

 Q Give three examples of showing internal LOC on the job.

400 POINTS
LOCUS OF CONTROL

 Q What kind of LOC do we generally want you to have? Why?

300 POINTS
LOCUS OF CONTROL

 Q Give three examples of showing external LOC on the job.

400 POINTS
LOCUS OF CONTROL

 Q Does having an internal LOC mean you should take responsibility for something you did not do? Give an example of when this situation might occur on the job.

300 POINTS
LOCUS OF CONTROL

 Q Your coffee spills on the computer keyboard. Your boss is angry. How should you respond internally?

400 POINTS
LOCUS OF CONTROL

 *Making W.A.G.E.S. Game Cards*

A External, because luck is not controllable, and luck is something other than yourself.

A Example: "We increased production because we worked harder."

A External, because it sounds as though the person does not think s/he can influence the boss' opinion.

A A word, statement, or action that makes a person "go off" and begin to lose self-control.

A Examples: admitting you made a mistake; apologizing to a coworker; taking credit for your good work

A Internal.

A Examples: blaming your coworker; complaining about the boss; blaming success on luck

A Internal, because it shows you are willing to take credit or blame for what you do.

A Example: "I should not have had my coffee near the keyboard. I'm sorry. I won't do it again."

A No. Example: A coworker blames you for a mistake she made.

Q Role-play an example of you demonstrating external LOC: You are in a work situation where you are being criticized by a coworker for working slowly.

500 POINTS
LOCUS OF CONTROL

Q Name two qualities or characteristics of teamwork.

100 POINTS
TEAMWORK

Q Role-play an example of you demonstrating an internal LOC: You are in a work situation where your supervisor has accused you of stealing and you are innocent.

500 POINTS
LOCUS OF CONTROL

Q Name one way to show enthusiasm when working with others.

100 POINTS
TEAMWORK

Q Role-play an example of internal LOC involving coworkers who ignore you and will not talk to you, but you want to interact with them.

500 POINTS
LOCUS OF CONTROL

Q Why is having a team leader important?

100 POINTS
TEAMWORK

Q Role-play an external LOC work scenario of your choice, followed by the same scenario done using internal LOC.

500 POINTS
LOCUS OF CONTROL

Q What kind of LOC should you have when working as a team—internal or external?

100 POINTS
TEAMWORK

Q Define internal LOC, state whether it is "owning" or "moaning," and demonstrate you understand it by responding to the following: You are late to work. When you got in the car that morning you realized you had no gas. What do you tell your boss?

500 POINTS
LOCUS OF CONTROL

Q Why is it important to share ideas as a team?

100 POINTS
TEAMWORK

Making W.A.G.E.S. Game Cards

© The State of Oregon. User has permission to copy this page for classroom use.

A Examples: working together, patience, cooperation, leadership, trust, compromise.

A Example: "I'm working slow because you keep bugging me!"

A Examples: smiling, encouraging, sharing ideas.

A Example: "I did not take it, but I will help you look for it."

A Examples: guidance, so team members do not argue, to help process run smoothly.

A Example: Ask the coworkers why they ignore you, and try to talk about things they enjoy.

A Internal.

A Varies.

A Examples: to gather different perspectives; it is better to have many ideas to choose from in order to make the best choice.

A Taking personal credit or blame; "owning;" tell her you forgot to put gas in the car.

Q **Name four qualities or characteristics of teamwork.**

200 POINTS
TEAMWORK

Q **Name six qualities or characteristics of teamwork.**

300 POINTS
TEAMWORK

 Q **Why is asking questions important when working as a team?**

200 POINTS
TEAMWORK

Q **What do personal values have to do with teamwork?**

300 POINTS
TEAMWORK

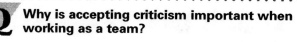 **Q** **Why is accepting criticism important when working as a team?**

200 POINTS
TEAMWORK

Q **What are four characteristics of a good team leader?**

300 POINTS
TEAMWORK

 Q **What is one role that someone on every team should fulfill?**

200 POINTS
TEAMWORK

Q **Define consensus.**

300 POINTS
TEAMWORK

 Q **What is creativity?**

200 POINTS
TEAMWORK

Q **Define assertiveness.**

300 POINTS
TEAMWORK

A Examples: working together, patience, cooperation, leadership, trust, compromise, respect, shared ideas.

A Examples: working together, patience, cooperation, leadership, trust, compromise.

A Team members must accept the opinions and values of others in order to reach agreement, and must be able to assert their own sets of values as a member of a team.

A Examples: avoid confusion, show interest, understand other team members.

A Examples: flexible, positive, organized, friendly, good communicator, gives directives without being too controlling.

A Examples: you can learn from others; improving yourself; showing self-control.

A When every member of a group is willing to go along with the general feeling of the group.

A Leader.

A An individual's ability to stand up for what they believe.

A Using your unique abilities to create something not everyone can easily create.

© The State of Oregon. User has permission to copy this page for classroom use.

Q **How can you demonstrate self-control when a team member (coworker) blames you for his or her mistake?**

400 POINTS
TEAMWORK

 Q **Name eight qualities or characteristics of teamwork.**

500 POINTS
TEAMWORK

 Q **Make two positive (and true) statements to members of your team.**

400 POINTS
TEAMWORK

 Q **Role-play working as a team in this scenario: The boss needs two trucks loaded within one hour.**

500 POINTS
TEAMWORK

 Q **You are a team leader at a work site. One member of the team keeps complaining. What do you do?**

400 POINTS
TEAMWORK

 Q **Role-play working as an effective leader of a team.**

500 POINTS
TEAMWORK

 Q **You work with a team of people who do not let you work on the jobs you are skilled at, even though you have told them you would do best on those parts. You really want to work on those parts of the job. What do you do?**

400 POINTS
TEAMWORK

 Q **Role-play a brainstorming session involving what your new business mission statement will be.**

500 POINTS
TEAMWORK

 Q **One of your coworkers slacks off when the boss is not around. Later, the boss gets angry at both of you for not getting your work done. What do you do?**

400 POINTS
TEAMWORK

 Q **Make four positive (and true) statements to members of your team.**

500 POINTS
TEAMWORK

Making *W.A.G.E.S.* Game Cards

A Examples: working together, patience, cooperation, leadership, trust, compromise, respect, shared ideas, helping others.

A Talk with the coworker privately and calmly about how this upsets you.

A Varies.

A Varies.

A Varies, but should include such qualities as being flexible, positive, organized, friendly, good communicator, etc.

A Take the member aside to talk and explain that the team needs encouragement, not negativity.

A Varies.

A Go to the team leader or boss to explain your case, and request to work on those parts of the jobs.

A Varies.

A Go to the coworker and politely ask him or her to work harder/more quickly.

Define one-way communication.

100 POINTS
COMMUNICATION

 What is the value of two-way communication?

200 POINTS
COMMUNICATION

 Define two-way communication.

100 POINTS
COMMUNICATION

 What does it mean to paraphrase?

200 POINTS
COMMUNICATION

 Give two examples of nonverbal communication.

100 POINTS
COMMUNICATION

 Why is asking questions important when communicating with your boss or coworkers?

200 POINTS
COMMUNICATION

 Give an example of showing enthusiasm on the job.

100 POINTS
COMMUNICATION

 Why is accepting criticism important on the job?

200 POINTS
COMMUNICATION

 Give two qualities or characteristics of good communication.

100 POINTS
COMMUNICATION

 What is an assertive communication style?

200 POINTS
COMMUNICATION

Making *W.A.G.E.S.* Game Cards

A Examples: possible to clarify what you've heard; two or more people working together to understand.

A When one person is doing all of the talking and others don't ask questions or interact with the person.

A It is a communication style in which you state in your own words what you think someone just said.

A When people interact, listen, and ask questions of one another to clearly understand what is said.

A Examples: clarifying, showing interest, avoiding making mistakes.

A Examples: eye contact, posture, arms crossed, smiling, frowning, tone of voice, stomping.

A Example: It can help you learn from those who have been there and improve your abilities.

A Examples: smiling, tone of voice, encouraging others, sharing ideas.

A When a person can communicate with assured strength and sensitivity.

A Examples: eye contact, smiling, body language, good posture, firm handshake, being nice to others, not interrupting, giving good feedback, being respectful, asking questions.

Define constructive communication and give an example.

300 POINTS
COMMUNICATION

 Come up with a team motto that reflects hope and optimism.

400 POINTS
COMMUNICATION

 Demonstrate/act out three ways of looking like an active listener.

300 POINTS
COMMUNICATION

 What is the main difference between "I" and "You" statements when it comes to LOC?

400 POINTS
COMMUNICATION

 Give three examples of an "invitation" to anger on the job.

300 POINTS
COMMUNICATION

 Role-play a good greeting at the beginning of an interview.

400 POINTS
COMMUNICATION

 Role-play three ways of looking like a poor listener.

300 POINTS
COMMUNICATION

 Role-play the following: Your boss tells you a number of tasks you need to complete, and you clarify his directions by asking questions.

400 POINTS
COMMUNICATION

 Should an interviewee ask questions at the end of an interview? Why or why not?

300 POINTS
COMMUNICATION

Role-play answering this interview question as though it is the end of an interview: Do you have any questions for me?

400 POINTS
COMMUNICATION

Making *W.A.G.E.S.* Game Cards

A Varies.

A This is communication that involves trying to understand and appreciate other people's points of view. For example, two coworkers who have been arguing about which one of them caused a machine to break down decide to repair it together.

A "I" statements suggest an internal LOC, while "You" statements suggest an external LOC.

A Examples: eye contact, leaning forward, asking questions, paraphrasing, showing emotion.

A Should include such things as strong handshake, smiling, eye contact, introduce self, etc.

A Examples: someone pulls your hair; coworker blames you for his mistake; someone yells at you; boss tells you to redo your work.

A Examples: Which do you want me to do first? Can I write these tasks down before you leave?

A Examples: arms crossed, looking down or away, interrupting, fidgeting, talking about other things.

A Responds by asking at least one appropriate question.

A Yes, to show interest, clarify, show you have researched the company, etc.

Q Role-play an interaction with your boss in which you use an "I" statement. Then do it again using a "You" statement.

500 POINTS
COMMUNICATION

 Q What are the four steps of the problem-solving strategy RADD?

100 POINTS
PROBLEM SOLVING

 Q Role-play a situation in which you use self-control skills: A coworker taunts you.

500 POINTS
COMMUNICATION

 Q At least how many alternatives should you generate for a problem?

100 POINTS
PROBLEM SOLVING

 Q Role-play a work situation that demonstrates your ability to accept criticism.

500 POINTS
COMMUNICATION

 Q Define "problem."

100 POINTS
PROBLEM SOLVING

 Q Role-play these interview questions: (1) What strengths do you have related to this job? (2) Tell me about your experience with this type of work (make up a type of job).

500 POINTS
COMMUNICATION

 Q Must you always decide on only one of your RADD alternatives? Why or why not?

100 POINTS
PROBLEM SOLVING

 Q You want a raise. Role-play how you effectively could communicate this to your boss.

500 POINTS
COMMUNICATION

 Q Define honesty as it relates to the workplace.

100 POINTS
PROBLEM SOLVING

A Recognize the problem (from all angles), generate Alternatives, Decide on an alternative or two, Determine if it was the right decision.

A Varies.

A Three.

A Varies.

A Any time a difficult situation occurs where there is no clear solution.

A Varies.

A No, because you might be able to try more than one alternative at once and be more effective.

A Varies.

A The measure of how much a person is truthful to and respectful of coworkers and supervisors.

A Example: Make an appointment with him or her. Then explain you have worked there for six months and have done well, and you feel you deserve a raise.

Q Define dependability as it relates to the workplace.

200 POINTS
PROBLEM SOLVING

Q Give two examples of harassment you might experience on the job.

300 POINTS
PROBLEM SOLVING

Q Why is it important to be honest on the job?

200 POINTS
PROBLEM SOLVING

Q What could an emotional reaction to the following problem be: Your coworker constantly criticizes you for your work.

300 POINTS
PROBLEM SOLVING

Q Share a recent problem one of your team members had to solve. Tell how that team member solved it.

200 POINTS
PROBLEM SOLVING

Q Define enthusiasm as it relates to the workplace, and give an example of how to show it.

300 POINTS
PROBLEM SOLVING

Q Why is it important not to just react to a problem you are confronted with?

200 POINTS
PROBLEM SOLVING

Q Your boss tells you what to do to begin a new task, then leaves. You did not fully understand him. What can you do?

300 POINTS
PROBLEM SOLVING

Q Why is it important to recognize a problem from the other people's perspective as well as your own?

200 POINTS
PROBLEM SOLVING

Q The boss feels he cannot rely upon you. This means he does not think you are ____.

300 POINTS
PROBLEM SOLVING

A Examples: sexual, violence, picking on you.

A The measure of how much a person can be relied upon by coworkers and supervisors to perform work-related tasks.

A Examples: yell at her; hit her; criticize her back.

A Examples: You could get fired; people will lose respect for you; to demonstrate you are responsible.

A The measure of how much a person enjoys his or her work and expresses that enjoyment appropriately to others. You can show it by smiling, offering new ideas, having a positive attitude, etc.

A Varies.

A Find the boss and clarify his instructions before starting the job.

A You often will react emotionally, not logically, without thinking through the most effective response.

A Dependable.

A So you can decide on an alternative or two that will be the least likely to cause even more problems, and will be most likely to satisfy both people or both sides.

Q Your boss asks you why you have been late the past few days. Give an honest answer without blaming someone or something else.

400 POINTS
PROBLEM SOLVING

 Q Role-play the following: A coworker punches you in the arm to get your attention, and you respond by dealing appropriately with the situation.

500 POINTS
PROBLEM SOLVING

 Q You need a day off from work in two weeks. How do you go about asking for it?

400 POINTS
PROBLEM SOLVING

 Q RADD the following problem: You have moved 20 miles from your workplace and have no car. You need to be to work by 8:00 a.m. This job is very important to you.

500 POINTS
PROBLEM SOLVING

 Q Recognize the following problem from both your and your boss' perspectives: It is the busiest day of the year for the business you work in. You feel very sick and ask to go home. The boss denies your request.

400 POINTS
PROBLEM SOLVING

 Q RADD the following problem: You are tired & want to leave your job early. You tell your boss you are sick, and then you leave. The boss later finds out you weren't sick and becomes very angry.

500 POINTS
PROBLEM SOLVING

 Q Recognize the following problem from both your and your boss' perspectives: You are told by your boss you cannot wear shorts on the job. You don't think she had the right to tell you how to dress.

400 POINTS
PROBLEM SOLVING

 Q RADD the following problem: You are working in a restaurant that is extremely busy. You are a waiter/waitress. Your boss seems to yell at you constantly to keep moving, but he seems not to yell at your coworkers. You think you are being singled out because you are new, although you feel you are doing a great job.

500 POINTS
PROBLEM SOLVING

 Q Recognize the following problem from both your and your boss' perspectives: You are a school janitor. One afternoon your boss tells you to clean the bathrooms again because they weren't satisfactorily cleaned. You are exhausted and think you did a fine job the first time.

400 POINTS
PROBLEM SOLVING

 Q RADD the following problem: You have been at your current job for one year. You are offered a new job that pays more, but you must start right away. You tell your boss that tomorrow is your last day. Your boss responds by getting angry and telling you that you must give two weeks notice before quitting.

500 POINTS
PROBLEM SOLVING

A Award points based on teacher discretion.

A Examples: I have been turning off my alarm; I have been going to bed too late.

A Award points based on teacher discretion.

A Examples: file a written request; follow workplace policy.

A Award points based on teacher discretion.

A Award points based on teacher discretion.

A Award points based on teacher discretion.

A Award points based on teacher discretion.

A Award points based on teacher discretion.

A Award points based on teacher discretion.

UNIT MASTERY VOCABULARY TESTS

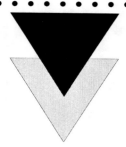

Name:_____

Unit One

Mastery Vocabulary Test

From the Choices column, write the word or phrase that best labels the definition/example. You may use a word more than one time.

ANSWER	DEFINITION		CHOICES
	A measure of how little self-control and responsibility a person has for his or her own behavior; people that tend to moan about, or place credit or blame for, their actions have this.	A	INTERNAL LOCUS OF CONTROL
	A measure that determines how much self-control and responsibility a person has for his or her own behavior; people that tend to own, or take credit or blame for, their actions have this.	B	AFFIRMATION
	Having a thought like, "I am liked by my fellow employees," after your boss criticizes your work.	C	COOLING OFF
	Physical/emotional indicators like sweaty palms, clenched fists, a red face, tight stomach, elevated breathing, or a suffocating feeling.	D	PROP
	Taking on the role of an angry student who makes excuses about not doing his/her homework.	E	EXTERNAL LOCUS OF CONTROL
	Tending to moan about or place blame for your actions, like whining or making excuses about being late.	F	FIRECRACKER
	Tending to own or take the credit or blame for one's actions.	G	PARAPHRASE
	The physical/emotional indicators that signify someone is under stress and losing control.	H	LOCUS OF CONTROL
	To act out a situation, behavior or attitude as if it were really happening.	I	PRESSURE GAUGE
	What someone does to get things back under control.	J	ROLE-PLAY
	Being called "stupid" by a coworker might be this.	K	"YOU" MESSAGES

SCORE: _____ /11

Name:_____

Unit One

Mastery Vocabulary Test

Answer Sheet

From the Choices column, write the word or phrase that best labels the definition/example. You may use a word more than one time.

ANSWER	DEFINITION		CHOICES
E External Locus of Control	A measure of how little self-control and responsibility a person has for his or her own behavior; people that tend to moan about, or place credit or blame for, their actions have this.	A	INTERNAL LOCUS OF CONTROL
A Internal Locus of Control	A measure that determines how much self-control and responsibility a person has for his or her own behavior; people that tend to own, or take credit or blame for, their actions have this.	B	AFFIRMATION
B Affirmation	Having a thought like, "I am liked by my fellow employees," after your boss criticizes your work.	C	COOLING OFF
I Pressure Gauge	Physical/emotional indicators like sweaty palms, clenched fists, a red face, tight stomach, elevated breathing, or a suffocating feeling.	D	PROP
J Role-Play	Taking on the role of an angry student who makes excuses about not doing his/her homework.	E	EXTERNAL LOCUS OF CONTROL
E External Locus of Control	Tending to moan about or place blame for your actions, like whining or making excuses about being late.	F	FIRECRACKER
A Internal Locus of Control	Tending to own or take the credit or blame for one's actions.	G	PARAPHRASE
I Pressure Gauge	The physical/emotional indicators that signify someone is under stress and losing control.	H	LOCUS OF CONTROL
J Role-Play	To act out a situation, behavior or attitude as if it were really happening.	I	PRESSURE GAUGE
C Cooling Off	What someone does to get things back under control.	J	ROLE PLAY
F Firecracker	Being called "stupid" by a coworker might be this.	K	"YOU" MESSAGES

SCORE: _____/11

Name:_____

Unit Two

Mastery Vocabulary Test

From the Choices column, write the word or phrase that best labels the definition/example. You may use a word more than one time.

ANSWER	DEFINITION		CHOICES
	An article used in a skit/play to make the setting or action seem more realistic.	A	SELF-ADVOCACY
	A person's ability to speak up, defend, or promote his or her opinion or belief.	B	ROLE-PLAY
	When every member of a group is willing to go along with the general feeling of the group.	C	CONSENSUS
	Talking to a supervisor about being sexually harassed by a coworker.	D	EXTERNAL LOCUS OF CONTROL
	Ted didn't particularly agree with his two friends, but they were so excited that he went along with their desires.	E	PROP
	An eye patch worn to define the role of a pirate, or a tie-dyed shirt to define the role of a 60's hippie.	F	INTERNAL LOCUS OF CONTROL
	Being able to let a coworker know they are letting down the team by being late to work.	G	LOCUS OF CONTROL
	One of the items contained in the paper bag that provided support to the skit that your team performed.	H	PRESSURE GAUGE
		I	FIRECRACKER

SCORE: _____/8

Name: _____

Unit Two

Mastery Vocabulary Test
Answer Sheet

From the Choices column, write the word or phrase that best labels the definition/example. You may use a word more than one time.

ANSWER	DEFINITION		CHOICES
E Prop	An article used in a skit/play to make the setting or action seem more realistic.	A	SELF-ADVOCACY
A Self-Advocacy	A person's ability to speak up, defend, or promote his or her opinion or belief.	B	ROLE-PLAY
C Consensus	When every member of a group is willing to go along with the general feeling of the group.	C	CONSENSUS
A Self-Advocacy	Talking to a supervisor about being sexually harassed by a coworker.	D	EXTERNAL LOCUS OF CONTROL
C Consensus	Ted didn't particularly agree with his two friends, but they were so excited that he went along with their desires.	E	PROP
E Prop	An eye patch worn to define the role of a pirate, or a tie-dyed shirt to define the role of a 60's hippie.	F	INTERNAL LOCUS OF CONTROL
A Self-Advocacy	Being able to let a coworker know they are letting down the team by being late to work.	G	LOCUS OF CONTROL
E Prop	One of the items contained in the paper bag that provided support to the skit that your team performed.	H	PRESSURE GAUGE
		I	FIRECRACKER

SCORE: _____ /8

Name:_____

Unit Three

Mastery Vocabulary Test

From the Choices column, write the word or phrase that best labels the definition/example. You may use a word more than one time.

ANSWER	DEFINITION		CHOICES
	A communication style where you state in your own words what you thought someone just said.	A	VENT
	A response that reflects moaning, blaming, or whining.	B	TWO-WAY COMMUNICATION
	A response that reflects owning, responsibility, or self-control.	C	PASSIVE COMMUNICATION STYLE
	An attitude that allows one to see the bright side in situations.	D	PARAPHRASE
	Being able to respond with a positive attitude to a supervisor, coworker, or customer who wants something done differently.	E	OPTIMISM
	Information that is provided as a response to an action, event, or behavior that can be used to create improvement or change.	F	ONE-WAY COMMUNICATION
	Statements that are used to express opinions, thoughts, or feelings and that tend to represent statements of ownership.	G	NONVERBAL COMMUNICATION
	Statements that tend to express opinions, thoughts, or feelings through whining and blaming others.	H	INTERVIEWER
	The measure of how much a person enjoys his or her work, and expresses that enjoyment appropriately to others.	I	INTERVIEWEE
	The person who conducts the job interview.	J	INTERNAL RESPONSE
	The person who seeks the job and must answer questions in order to be evaluated by the interviewer.	K	GREETING
	The way an interviewee introduces himself or herself to an interviewer.	L	FEEDBACK
	To be able to see things from the other person's perspective.	M	EXTERNAL RESPONSE
	To get things "off one's chest."	N	ENTHUSIASM

Unit Three
Mastery Vocabulary Test
(continued)

ANSWER	DEFINITION		CHOICES
	What an individual says with his or her body, facial expressions, tone of voice, and posture.	O	EMPATHY
	When a person can communicate with assured strength and sensitivity.	P	ASSERTIVE COMMUNICATION STYLE
	When a person gives the impression that everything is okay, even when it is not.	Q	AGGRESSIVE COMMUNICATION STYLE
	When a person states how they feel and think without considering the feelings of others.	R	ACCEPTING CRITICISM
	When one person is doing all of the talking and others don't ask questions or interact with the person.	S	"YOU" MESSAGES
	When people interact, listen, and ask questions of one another to clearly understand what is said.	T	"I" MESSAGES

SCORE: _____/20

Name:_____

Unit Three

Mastery Vocabulary Test
Answer Sheet

From the Choices column, write the word or phrase that best labels the definition/example. You may use a word more than one time.

ANSWER	DEFINITION		CHOICES
D Paraphrase	A communication style where you state in your own words what you thought someone just said.	A	VENT
M External Response	A response that reflects moaning, blaming, or whining.	B	TWO-WAY COMMUNICATION
J Internal Response	A response that reflects owning, responsibility, or self-control.	C	PASSIVE COMMUNICATION STYLE
E Optimism	An attitude that allows one to see the bright side in situations.	D	PARAPHRASE
R Accepting Criticism	Being able to respond with a positive attitude to a supervisor, coworker, or customer who wants something done differently.	E	OPTIMISM
L Feedback	Information that is provided as a response to an action, event, or behavior that can be used to create improvement or change.	F	ONE-WAY COMMUNICATION
T "I" Messages	Statements that are used to express opinions, thoughts, or feelings and that tend to represent statements of ownership.	G	NONVERBAL COMMUNICATION
S "You" Messages	Statements that tend to express opinions, thoughts, or feelings through whining and blaming others.	H	INTERVIEWER
N Enthusiasm	The measure of how much a person enjoys his or her work, and expresses that enjoyment appropriately to others.	I	INTERVIEWEE
H Interviewer	The person who conducts the job interview.	J	INTERNAL RESPONSE
I Interviewee	The person who seeks the job and must answer questions in order to be evaluated by the interviewer.	K	GREETING

Unit Three
Mastery Vocabulary Test
Answers
(continued)

Answer	Definition		Choices
K Greeting	The way an interviewee introduces himself or herself to an interviewer.	L	Feedback
O Empathy	To be able to see things from the other person's perspective.	M	External Response
A Vent	To get things "off one's chest."	N	Enthusiasm
G Nonverbal Communication	What an individual says with his or her body, facial expressions, tone of voice, and posture.	O	Empathy
P Assertive Communication Style	When a person can communicate with assured strength and sensitivity.	P	Assertive Communication Style
C Passive Communication Style	When a person gives the impression that everything is okay, even when it is not.	Q	Aggressive Communication Style
Q Aggressive Communication Style	When a person states how they feel and think without considering the feelings of others.	R	Accepting Criticism
F One-Way Communication	When one person is doing all of the talking and others don't ask questions or interact with the person.	S	"You" messages
B Two-Way Communication	When people interact, listen, and ask questions of one another to clearly understand what is said.	T	"I" messages

Score: _____/20

Name:_____

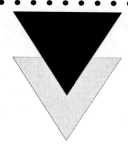

Unit Four

Mastery Vocabulary Test

From the Choices column, write the word or phrase that best labels the definition/example. You may use a word more than one time.

Answer	Definition		Choices
	Potential solutions to solving the problem.	A	Alternatives
	A sense or feeling of ownership that leads one to act in a dependable manner.	B	Confess
	Any time a difficult situation occurs where there is no clear solution.	C	Consensus
	The measure of how much a person can be relied upon by coworkers and supervisors to perform work-related tasks.	D	Dependability
	The first step in using the RADD problem-solving technique involves recognizing the _____.	E	Exaggeration
	Another way of saying "on time." For example, showing up for work, meetings, and events before they begin.	F	Honesty
	A personal quality that a person possesses that creates a strong sense of faith and trust in their character.	G	Problem
	Stretching the truth to make a favorable impression.	H	Punctuality
	The act of admitting a mistake or accepting responsibility for an error.	I	Responsibility
	Your boss knows that he can count on you to be on time for meetings because of this quality.	J	Role-Play
	Admitting to mistakes and demonstrating an internal locus of control.	K	Self-Advocacy

Score: _____11

Name: _____

Unit Four

Mastery Vocabulary Test

Answer Sheet

From the Choices column, write the word or phrase that best labels the definition/example. You may use a word more than one time.

ANSWER	DEFINITION		CHOICES
A **Alternatives**	Potential solutions to solving the problem.	**A**	ALTERNATIVES
I **Responsibility**	A sense or feeling of ownership that leads one to act in a dependable manner.	**B**	CONFESS
G **Problem**	Any time a difficult situation occurs where there is no clear solution.	**C**	CONSENSUS
D **Dependability**	The measure of how much a person can be relied upon by coworkers and supervisors to perform work-related tasks.	**D**	DEPENDABILITY
G **Problem**	The first step in using the RADD problem-solving technique involves recognizing the _____.	**E**	EXAGGERATION
H **Punctuality**	Another way of saying "on time." For example, showing up for work, meetings, and events before they begin.	**F**	HONESTY
F **Honesty**	A personal quality that a person possesses that creates a strong sense of faith and trust in their character.	**G**	PROBLEM
E **Exaggeration**	Stretching the truth to make a favorable impression.	**H**	PUNCTUALITY
B **Confess**	The act of admitting a mistake or accepting responsibility for an error.	**I**	RESPONSIBILITY
H **Punctuality**	Your boss knows that he can count on you to be on time for meetings because of this quality.	**J**	ROLE-PLAY
B **Confess**	Admitting to mistakes and demonstrating an internal locus of control.	**K**	SELF-ADVOCACY

SCORE: _____/11

EMPLOYER
MOCK
INTERVIEW
EVALUATON

Employer Mock Interview
Evaluation

PRESENTATION

PERSONAL APPEARANCE (HYGIENE, GROOMING, APPROPRIATE DRESS)

Hygiene: *Applicant's hair, skin, teeth, nails, and clothes are all very clean.*

5	4	3	2	1
OUTSTANDING		AVERAGE		UNACCEPTABLE

Grooming: *Applicant's hair is combed/styled, nails are trimmed/manicured appropriately, and face is clean-shaven or facial hair is trimmed properly.*

5	4	3	2	1
OUTSTANDING		AVERAGE		UNACCEPTABLE

Appropriate Dress: *Applicant's clothes fit properly and are appropriate for a serious job interview, no inappropriate hairstyles, clothing accessories, or body piercing.*

5	4	3	2	1
OUTSTANDING		AVERAGE		UNACCEPTABLE

PROPER GREETING, INTRODUCTION, AND CLOSING

Proper Greeting: *Applicant walks into interview smiling, tall and confident, waits for interviewer to initiate greeting, and responds appropriately (e.g., "I'm pleased to meet you").*

5	4	3	2	1
OUTSTANDING		AVERAGE		UNACCEPTABLE

Introduction: *Applicant greets interviewer with eye contact, smile, firm handshake, clear introduction of name, and waits to be invited by interviewer to sit.*

5	4	3	2	1
OUTSTANDING		AVERAGE		UNACCEPTABLE

Closing: *Applicant closes interview by engaging interviewer with direct eye contact, smile, firm handshake, and statement of thanks for the opportunity to interview.*

5	4	3	2	1
OUTSTANDING		AVERAGE		UNACCEPTABLE

POISE, MATURITY, AND ATTITUDE

Poise: *Applicant sits upright and comfortably, facing the interviewer in a relaxed, open manner, and keeps nervous habits (e.g., fidgeting with rings, pens, hands) to a minimum.*

5	4	3	2	1
OUTSTANDING		AVERAGE		UNACCEPTABLE

Maturity: *Applicant lets interviewer start interview by asking first question or by initiating small talk, and throughout interview waits for interviewer to finish talking before speaking/answering.*

5	4	3	2	1
OUTSTANDING		AVERAGE		UNACCEPTABLE

Attitude: *Applicant conducts self in a professional manner by being polite, courteous, friendly, and using good manners.*

5	4	3	2	1
OUTSTANDING		AVERAGE		UNACCEPTABLE

INTERVIEW

SELF-CONFIDENCE, INITIATIVE, AND ASSERTIVENESS

Self-Confident: *Applicant speaks clearly about interests, strengths, and abilities, accepts responsibility for self, and does not make derogatory comments about present or former employers or coworkers.*

5	4	3	2	1
OUTSTANDING		AVERAGE		UNACCEPTABLE

Initiative: *Applicant shows initiative through verbal (speaks with enthusiasm, asks appropriate questions) and nonverbal (leans forward on occasion, nods to show interest/active listening) aspects of answers.*

5	4	3	2	1
OUTSTANDING		AVERAGE		UNACCEPTABLE

Assertiveness: *Applicant presents personal characteristics/qualifications in a positive, confident manner without "overselling" or indicating a "know it all" attitude.*

5	4	3	2	1
OUTSTANDING		AVERAGE		UNACCEPTABLE

COMMUNICATION SKILLS, BOTH VERBAL AND NON-VERBAL

Verbal Skills: *Applicant keeps answers short, to the point, and in complete sentences; speaks fluently and keeps use of slang (e.g., "like") and halting speech (e.g., "uh" "er" "well") to a minimum, and uses voice tone and inflection that shows enthusiasm and interest.*

5	4	3	2	1
OUTSTANDING		AVERAGE		UNACCEPTABLE

Nonverbal Skills: *Applicant uses body language (e.g., smiling, maintaining eye contact, nodding, leaning forward, using hand gestures) to show active listening, interest, and enthusiasm.*

5	4	3	2	1
OUTSTANDING		AVERAGE		UNACCEPTABLE

Verbal and Nonverbal Together: *Applicant creates as close a match as possible between verbal and nonverbal behavior whenever appropriate (e.g., answering a question about interests by speaking with enthusiasm while leaning forward or using hand gestures to reinforce words being spoken).*

5	4	3	2	1
OUTSTANDING		AVERAGE		UNACCEPTABLE

CAREER KNOWLEDGE, CAREER PLANS, AND JOB QUALIFICATIONS

Career Knowledge: *Applicant shows through answers/conversation a basic understanding of job and training options in the career path he/she has selected.*

5	4	3	2	1
OUTSTANDING		AVERAGE		UNACCEPTABLE

Career Plans: *Applicant shows a basic understanding of the work requirements in his/her selected career path by answering questions using concrete work or school-related examples when appropriate (e.g., using a personal work or school-related example to illustrate an answer to a question about skills needed on a job or about a hypothetical situation posed by the interviewer).*

5	4	3	2	1
OUTSTANDING		AVERAGE		UNACCEPTABLE

Job Qualifications: *Applicant demonstrates through interview that he/she has basic qualities important to any job/employer, including positive work attitude, willingness to learn, spirit of cooperation, ability to get along with others, and respect for employer.*

5	4	3	2	1
OUTSTANDING		AVERAGE		UNACCEPTABLE

APPLICATION MATERIALS

EFFECTIVENESS OF APPLICATION MATERIALS (E.G., RÉSUMÉ, APPLICATION LETTER)

Materials Complete: *Applicant identifies career interests, education background, work experiences, and work-related strengths and qualifications in his/her application materials.*

5	4	3	2	1
OUTSTANDING		AVERAGE		UNACCEPTABLE

Materials Professionally Prepared: *Applicant has prepared all materials in a professional manner (e.g., written clearly, used proper grammar, enough copies.)*

5	4	3	2	1
OUTSTANDING		AVERAGE		UNACCEPTABLE

SUMMARY OF INTERVIEW

To help this applicant in future interviews, please identify the greatest strength and the greatest area in need of improvement that you observed in the interview.

STRENGTH:

AREA OF IMPROVEMENT:

W.A.G.E.S.

Working at Gaining Employment Skills

**A Job-Related
Social Skills
Curriculum
for Adolescents**

Michael D. Johnson, M.Ed.

Michael Bullis, Ph.D.

Michael R. Benz, Ph.D.

Keith Hollenbeck, Ph.D.

ISBN 1-59318-068-3

09 08   6 5 4 3

Printed in the United States of America

Published and Distributed by

SOPRIS
WEST™
EDUCATIONAL SERVICES

A Cambium Learning™ Company

4093 Specialty Place • Longmont, Colorado 80504

(303) 651-2829 • www.sopriswest.com

220WAGES/10-05